# DIGITAL PIO
# SPIRIT

## Thomas A. Christie

# Other Books by Thomas A. Christie

# DIGITAL PIONEER SPIRIT

## The Freewheeling Creative Innovation of Mel Croucher on the Home Microcomputer

### Thomas A. Christie

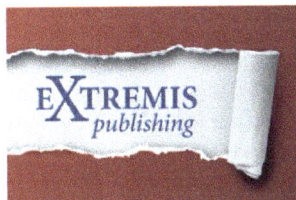

eXTREMIS
*publishing*

*Digital Pioneer Spirit: The Freewheeling Creative Innovation of Mel Croucher on the Home Microcomputer* by Thomas A. Christie.

First edition published in Great Britain in 2025 by Extremis Publishing Ltd., Suite 218, Castle House, 1 Baker Street, Stirling, FK8 1AL, United Kingdom.

*www.extremispublishing.com*

Extremis Publishing is a Private Limited Company registered in Scotland (SC509983) whose Registered Office is Suite 218, Castle House, 1 Baker Street, Stirling, FK8 1AL, United Kingdom.

A CIP catalogue record for this book is available from the British Library.

ISBN: 978-1-0682314-0-7

Typeset in Sorts Mill Goudy, designed by The League of Moveable Type.
Printed and bound in Great Britain by IngramSpark, Chapter House, Pitfield, Kiln Farm, Milton Keynes, MK11 3LW, United Kingdom.

# Contents

# Introduction

It's often said that if you can remember the 1960s and 1970s, you weren't really there. If you can remember the 1980s, on the other hand, then you will almost certainly recall the name of Mel Croucher. If you had even the most fleeting interest in home computing during the eighties, Mel Croucher was *everywhere*. Before anyone had even heard of Max Headroom, Croucher had already firmly established himself as Britain's first fully-realised multimedia personality, and—so great was his influence over digital culture—the inspiration of his boundless creative invention can still be felt even today.

No other single cultural figure has had nearly as much impact on the direction of my career over the years as Mel Croucher has done. I avidly followed his innovative work while growing up, and I have continued to do so throughout adult life. His constant originality still continues to amaze and inspire me. There has never been any other creative maverick quite like him, making his trailblazing work so distinctive that it is almost impossible to categorise. In many ways, his pioneering interdisciplinary approach has made him seem a bit like John von Neumann, Weird Al Yankovic, Salvador Dalí, and Kenny Everett rolled into one.

When, on the 19th of November 1977, Croucher established his software company Automata UK, little could he have realised that he would eventually become universally recognised as the father of the British computer games industry. First transmitting games over Radio Victory 257FM in December 1977, he was streaming digital entertainment decades before it became the norm (and, indeed, before most people had even considered the then-very-costly prospect of owning a home computer). This forward-thinking approach anticipated today's ubiquitous digital download and streaming culture by decades. When Sir Clive Sinclair unleashed his ZX Spectrum on an unsuspecting world a few years later, Automata Software was already an established veteran of the games industry just as affordable home computer technology was first coming into the hands of the wider public.

Croucher's career has been witness to a panoply of notable innovations. His anarchic recordings on computer magazine cover-mounted cassettes predated podcasts by more than a decade, while his text-based puzzle game *iD* would presage the large language models that have revolutionised the computing world in recent years. Arguably his most famous title, *Deus Ex Machina*, was so ahead of its time that it would eventually become one of the most analysed British computer games of the eighties—indeed, it remains of interest to commentators and academics even today, more than forty years later. His prolific writing career has spanned everything from regular columns to comic strips by way of instruction manuals and textbooks. He made frequent TV and radio appearances, both serious and comedic, and has become synonymous with the early digital age.

This is not a biography of Croucher's life—remarkable though that life has been. His acclaimed 2014 book, *Deus Ex Machina: The Best Game You Never Played in Your Life*, records his personal recollections of Automata UK's development and the company's indelible impact on the computer industry in the early eighties. Instead, this book aims to chronicle some aspect of his immense contribution to the world of computing and digital culture across the past five decades, considering his games, his writing, and his many other innovations which have emerged over the years.

Croucher has established himself as an undisputed master of narrative-driven digital experiences. He remains a unique figure in the intersection of technology, storytelling, and digital culture, having made significant and lasting contributions to the digital humanities over the years. His enduring impact is evident. As founder of Automata UK, Croucher created some of the first computer games ever to exhibit strong narrative and philosophical elements. He viewed games not just as entertainment but rather as an entirely new artistic medium, pushing the boundaries of what digital platforms could achieve. His work gleefully blurred the lines between gaming, performance art, and social commentary, helping to define computer games as a legitimate form of cultural expression within the digital humanities and beyond.

Croucher's work often contained satirical and critical reflections on society, technology, and human nature. Many of his games became noteworthy for their thoughtful undertones, questioning the extent of free will, the dangers of authoritarianism, and the impact of technology on humanity—a theme that seems especially prescient, given the nature of the artificial intelligence-driven modern world we live in. In a way, his skill-set has had just as much in common with an independent filmmaker and interactive fiction writer as it does with those of a computer programmer. Croucher's unique approach to game design and multimedia storytelling has influenced generations of developers, writers, and artists—most certainly including myself. His continual and uncompromising emphasis on artistic integrity triumphing over commercialism has resonated with game developers and digital artists across Britain and far beyond.

While Croucher has been the driver behind several noteworthy firsts, many of which will be explored in this book, this tells only part of the story of why he has come to be regarded with such affection by the computing world. His reputation as a quirky and down-to-earth figure is well-known, reflecting his independent spirit and indefatigable sense of humour. He has been unstintingly active in engaging with fans and fellow developers over the years, sharing his experiences and stories from the early days of video game development. Those who have met or interacted with Croucher often describe him as easygoing and candid, particularly in conversations about his contributions to gaming and digital culture. Regarded as friendly and approachable, especially within creative communities, Croucher has participated in many interviews, podcasts, and public events where he has consistently come across as open, witty, and passionate about his work and the computer industry in general. His unconventional approach to creativity and his role as a forerunner in game design always make him an entertaining and accessible personality to interact with, and he remains highly respected within the gaming industry for his ground-breaking contributions—not only during the early days of home computing, but also his more recent activity in and around digital culture.

Croucher's achievements have earned him a cult status within the industry, and he is recognised globally as a key individual in the field of digital storytelling. He has also been a long-time advocate for independent game development. Few people have made quite as profound or as lasting an impact on digital culture as Croucher has done. His legacy in the digital humanities lies in his revolutionary spirit—pushing digital media beyond mere entertainment into the realms of synergistic narration, exploration of the human condition, and artistic innovation. Of all the creative figures to emerge from the golden age of home computing, Mel Croucher is the one that has been remembered for a lifetime—and for good reason. His work remains special because he didn't just set out to make computer games: he turned them into an experimental art form where it seemed as though almost anything could happen... and very often did. In Croucher's world, computer technology made creative possibilities virtually endless, and this unbridled enthusiasm soon proved to be infectious amongst his many fans and followers.

Croucher consistently approached gaming as a medium for social commentary, avant-garde expression, storytelling—and yes, fun—pushing the limits of what digital entertainment could be. Long before gaming embraced cinematic narratives, he was a cross-media visionary, merging music, spoken word, and visuals into a seamless experience. This approach would pave the way for later story-driven games and experimental media. He didn't make simple, escapist games; he constructed multi-layered narratives that challenged players to think about their attitudes and preconceptions. His work was self-funded, experimental, and willing to take risks that larger companies wouldn't. This autonomous, rebellious mindset would foreshadow the rise of indie game development.

Many of the aspects of modern computing to be established by Croucher—multimedia storytelling, narrative-driven action, and socially-conscious game design—only became industry standards years later. He was so far ahead of his time that much of his creative brilliance wasn't fully appreciated in his 1980s heyday, and is only now being properly acknowledged and celebrated in retrospect. Today, Croucher's influence can be seen in everything from experimental digital art to multi-platform storytelling. His work is considered so distinctive because he treated games as more than entertainment—they were vehicles for thought, emotion, and artistic expression. His blend of commentary, humour, and technological innovation has ensured that his groundbreaking contributions remain unique, compelling, and enduringly impactful on the world of digital humanities.

# DIGITAL PIONEER SPIRIT

## Thomas A. Christie

# Automata Dreams: The Early Years

It seems hard to believe nowadays, given his towering reputation in digital culture, but Mel Croucher wasn't always involved in the software industry. Before he founded Automata UK in 1977, Croucher had already led a diverse career in architecture, broadcasting, and early computer science. He initially trained as an architect, became a partner at Pioneer Design of Stockholm (specialising in hyperbolic paraboloid tensile structures), and then went on to work for the firm of Sir William Halcrow and Partners where he was instrumental in designing projects for Sheikh Rashid bin Saeed al-Maktoum, the then-ruler of Dubai. While his passion for media and technology soon led him into radio and print journalism, the skills earned during his professional experiences in architecture would provide him with a firm foundation for his later, highly innovative work in video game design and his many multimedia projects.

During the late 1960s and early 1970s, he became involved in the world of independent broadcasting, producing radio shows and lending his talents to creative projects that combined music, storytelling, and (increasingly) emergent digital technologies. His interest in computing developed during this period, following an early dalliance with the notion of becoming a computer scientist in the mid-1960s, and he began experimenting with numerous ways to integrate computing with entertainment and user interaction.

By the mid-1970s, thanks to the gradual arrival of home computer systems, Croucher was pioneering early computer-based entertainment, most notably as a result of his work in data transmission via radio signals. Games could be recorded from radio broadcasts and then loaded onto computer by use of cassette tape. This was a formative precursor to what would later become the practice of digital distribution. His background in blending computing with creative media laid the foundation for Automata UK, which—when it was established in 1977—became known as one of the first British software publishers, and a games studio renowned for its inventive (and often somewhat eccentric) approach to the design of its products. The Greek term 'automata' can essentially be translated as 'self-acting', and indeed few companies of the era would prove to be quite as independent or fiercely free-thinking.

Prior to Automata UK's entry into the world of software, Croucher spearheaded a novel project that distributed audio recordings on cassette tape not for the purposes of publishing music, but rather for the provision of information. In the early 1970s, he led the way in the concept of selling tourism guides on cassette tape, which were designed to provide audio-directed tours for travellers. These taped guides were created for use in cars and other vehicles, offering (often humorous) narrated information about various historical sites, landmarks, and cultural points of interest within a certain area. These guides provided historical and informative commentary about the areas that tourists were visiting. The plan was that travellers could play these tapes while driving through specific locations, receiving real-time commentary about their surroundings—essentially a forerunner to modern GPS-based audio guides, and an early example of using recorded media to provide an interactional travel experience.

Croucher's work on these audio guides provided him with invaluable experience in blending storytelling, sound, and technology. This approach later influenced his transmedia approach to interactive entertainment when he made the transition into computer gaming and software development with Automata UK. He was joined in this endeavour by his friend and fellow entrepreneur Christian Penfold, a larger-than-life character who had originally advertised in the cassette guides but soon decided to collaborate in the audio-based tourism business. When Croucher eventually made the transition into computer software—and, specifically, videogaming—Penfold became his business partner at Automata UK, focusing on the company's marketing and operations. Together, they developed a reputation for creating quirky, unconventional, and often satirical computer games. Their work would soon prove to be well ahead of its time, blending storytelling, music, and interactivity in ways that were groundbreaking for the era. It's important to note that Penfold would become a significant figure in the software industry in his own right, and has worked with companies as varied as Potassium Frog and Valve Corporation, amongst others, in a variety of senior roles.

As technology advanced and home computers began to achieve greater mainstream consumer acceptance from the late 1970s, Croucher and Penfold saw unparalleled potential for the publication of digital entertainment. This led them to shift their business emphasis away from audio guides toward the exciting, but nascent and unpredictable, computer games industry. Croucher focused on game development and creative direction, with Penfold concentrating on business operations, but the restrictive technology of the time meant that their work was cut out for them—games could initially take up no more than 1Kb of space, as that was all that many systems of the time could offer.

Croucher and Penfold were in agreement when it came to Automata UK's principles of game design: their titles would be strictly non-violent in nature (in stark contrast to the majority of other games available at the time), would challenge players to think as well as be entertained, and would also be unconventional and imaginative. These creditable principles were adhered to throughout the entire lifetime of the company. Between Automata UK's foundation in 1977 and its closure in 1985, over sixty titles were produced for a variety of different platforms. Initially, simple games were produced and transmitted over radio for systems like the Commodore PET, which boasted 4Kb of RAM (though some variants had up to 96Kb on board). Due to the limited graphical capabilities of these systems, the games tended to be predominantly text-based, but Croucher saw this more as a challenge than a limitation. The games he produced, including *The Pathfinder Quests* (1977–1980), *Whitbread Quiz Time* (1979) and *The Computer Treasure Hunt* (1979), often employed virtual puzzles which had real-world rewards: there were surprises in store for gamers savvy enough to unravel Croucher's cryptic clues and track down the prize. This innovation helped Automata to earn a cult following, even in the early days when computer ownership was still a prohibitively pricey prospect.

Automata UK found its unlikely headquarters in the form of Dorothy's Wool Shop in Southsea's 27 Highland Road, Portsmouth. (At time of writing, this commercial premises now houses an independent dental surgery.) The small but highly effective business team consisted of Croucher (the Managing Director) and his business partner, the marketing supremo, Penfold; graphic artist Robin 'Gremlin' Evans; in-house programmer Andrew Stagg; and the enigmatically-monikered 'Lady Claire Sinclive' (the alias of Carol Anne Wright) who was responsible for public relations and office management. As the company's cult credentials grew, so did the reputation of the staff members for

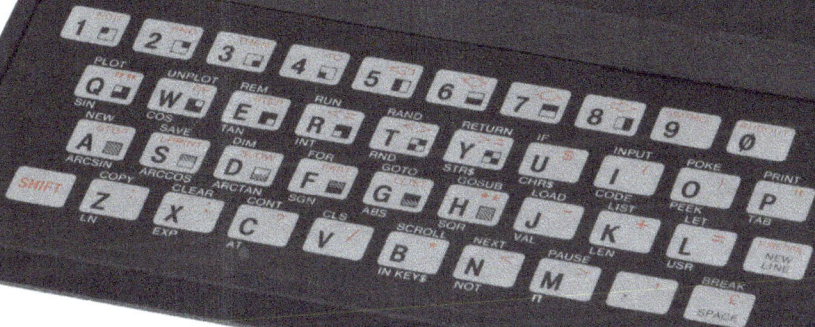

eccentric brilliance, and they collectively became the stuff of legends in computing circles—a welcome familiarity which Croucher would skilfully use to Automata's advantage when it came to later public appearances and in wider publicity strategies.

When Sir Clive Sinclair released his ZX80 and ZX81 microcomputers in 1980 and '81 respectively, a new era of cost-effective home computing had arrived... and Automata UK was ready. Already boasting a capacity for cassette recording thanks to Croucher's successful travel guide business, the company was well-prepared for this new era of home computing. The public uptake of these early systems, coupled with their use of cassette tape for data storage, meant that there was a large untapped audience out there in the UK just waiting for the arrival of computer-based entertainment. In spite of both systems' limited graphical capabilities and memory capacity (both had 1Kb of onboard RAM, though the ZX80 could be expanded to 16Kb and the ZX81 to a comparatively whopping 64Kb), Automata already had considerable experience under its belt at producing games which made the very most of modest system specifications. Compilations of affordable mini-games, produced on cassette tape and distributed via mail-order, soon proved to be a huge commercial hit for the company.

In 1982, Sinclair produced the ZX Spectrum for the first time—and while early models sported just 16Kb of RAM, its most famous iteration came with 48Kb onboard... a veritable powerhouse for the comparatively modest price of £125 or £175 respectively. Better yet, while the early Sinclair computers had only offered monochrome graphics, the Spectrum could display a 15 colour palette. Though Automata would release games for other platforms such as the Commodore 64, MSX, and Dragon 32, it is for their range of Spectrum titles that they will almost certainly be most fondly remembered, and throughout the system's early years the company produced a prolific output of games including *Spectrum Spectacular* (1983), *Bunny* (1983), *Morris Meets the Bikers* (1984), *Crusoe* (1984), and *New Wheels, John?* (1985). However—as we shall see in the coming chapters—it was ultimately Croucher's own titles that would prove to be the company's most instantly memorable amongst the general public.

Automata UK's visibility continued to increase, driven by its eye-catching cartoon-strip adverts (boasting narrative continuity), highly distinctive—and often riotous—appearances at trade fairs, and public awareness which was gradually heightened by Croucher's growing cult status and participation in the impressively riotous premium phone service *Mel Croucher's Computer Fun Line*, as well as press interest surrounding a Sunday newspaper's exposé of supposedly adult content in the company's early games (a claim robustly denied by Croucher) and a high-profile legal dispute with a famous board game manufacturer. However, the company became especially well-known for two particular qualities which stood out from the competition. Firstly, Croucher made novel use of the cassette tapes used to distribute Automata UK games; the program was stored on the A-side of the tape, while original music (performed by Croucher himself) was recorded on the B-side. This not only provided consumers with value for money, but also exposed the general public to his admirably unique musical style into the bargain. In an especially clever twist, the songs sometimes contained hints for the games they were bundled with. This strategy would subsequently be used by other software houses in later years, such as Trevor Lever and Peter Jones' *Dodgy Geezers* for Melbourne House (1986) and Mike Berry's song *Everyone's a Wally* (1985) which accompanied Mikro-Gen's famous action-adventure game of the same name.

However, the most instantly-recognisable aspect of Automata was almost certainly their mascot, the infamous PiMan. A good-natured, bright pink humanoid creature with a pendulous proboscis and the Greek character $\pi$ on his chest, the PiMan became the unlikely star of many of the company's titles. First appearing in the text adventure *PiMania* (1982), and created by Croucher and Penfold, the character would later appear in numerous games authored by other programmers including *Piballed* (1984), *Pi-Eyed* (1984), *Pi-in-'ere* (1984), *Piromania* (1984), and *OlymPiMania* (1984). Artist Robin Evans produced countless PiMan cartoons, many of which accompanied the company's advertising and publicity materials, and eventually the character was joined by a growing number of fellow Pi-People (including Swettibitz and Morris). The PiMan was immediately associated with Automata, and the character regularly made public appearances at live events (often portrayed by a costumed Penfold). The PiMan even appeared in two music albums, *The PiMan's Greatest Hits* (1983) and *The PiMan's Greatest Hits Too* (1985), with a subsequent re-release decades later in 2010 (on suitably retro vinyl LPs).

Today, Automata UK is remembered as one of the all-time classic British software houses of the 1970s and '80s, and the PiMan remains every bit as immortalised as other beloved Spectrum cultural icons such as Monty Mole, Miner Willy, Dizzy, Horace, Sabreman, and Magic Knight. The company was cherished by the public and the industry press alike for its quirkiness, invention, and incredible flair for marketing. But behind the mad songs, mind-bending puzzles, and crazy prize giveaways was a lasting creative legacy that would inspire countless game designers, artists, writers, musicians, and dreamers of all kinds. What exactly was it about Croucher's games in particular, then, that would make them stand out amongst not only the company's other well-regarded titles, but in the wider and increasingly competitive world of home computer games more generally?

# Can of Worms (1981)

An early but commercially successful release for Automata UK was *Can of Worms*, a compilation of mini-games which followed a format that would come to inform several of the company's later titles. Like many programmers faced with the prospect of cramming a playable experience into 1Kb of RAM for the newly-released Sinclair ZX81, Croucher viewed the situation not as a limitation but rather as a test of imagination. Similarly, with the machine's monochrome graphical capability meaning that the capacity for imagery was essentially reduced to ASCII text characters, using this rudimentary foundation for entertaining game design was always going to be an uphill struggle. Yet somehow, Croucher not only managed to overcome these hurdles but actually ended up creating a degree of unintentional controversy in the process.

Though a somewhat obscure entry amongst Automata's catalogue of titles today, *Can of Worms* remains a fascinating curiosity that reflected—even at this very early stage—Croucher's signature approach to digital media. Released for the ZX81, which was a significant but rudimentary computer system with very constrained capabilities, *Can of Worms* was not a straightforward game in the traditional sense. Rather, it was more of a participatory experience designed to provoke thought rather than offer conventional entertainment. It marked a diversion—and, arguably, an evolution—away from his earlier Commodore PET titles, in that it mixed experimental gameplay, social commentary, and unconventional storytelling to produce something that felt genuinely original for the time.

While nowadays we have become used to the concept of the mini-game compilation, not least thanks to consoles such as the Nintendo DS and Nintendo Wii where such titles became enormously popular in commercial terms, in the early days of microcomputing the idea was was still fresh and untried. Unlike the seminal arcade-style games of the same period, *Can of Worms* was an abstract simulation with very simple graphics that engaged players in a thought-provoking exercise, incorporating Croucher's trademark elements of satire, unpredictability, and player-driven decision-making.

As its title suggests, *Can of Worms* was a metaphorical exploration of opening up complex issues, whether political, social, or personal. Croucher became known for embedding subversive and thought-provoking themes in his games, often challenging players to reconsider their assumptions rather than merely providing the type of objective-based challenge common to other games of this era, and the *Can of Worms* allegory was certainly apposite given the eyebrow-raisingly unconventional topics raised by some of the individual mini-games themselves. Released so early in the company's history that it was still trading as Automata Cartography—a nod to Croucher's start in travel guides—it certainly proved to be a title which demanded public attention.

A glance at the typewritten cassette inlay revealed a line-up of mini-games so bafflingly abstruse, it's nothing short of a miracle that the compilation went largely unnoticed by the trade press of the time. In *Acne*, we witness Frankenstein's Monster as we have rarely seen him before—covered in facial pustules. The player must use the cursor keys to squeeze as many zits as possible within 100 seconds (essentially a game of whack-a-mole with pimples). Then, in *Vasectomy*, the challenge is to control the hands of an inebriated and short-sighted surgeon as they administer 'the snip' to a spectacularly unfortunate patient/victim. Some very careful timing will be required to carry out the procedure with any degree of accuracy... a task not helped by a constantly shifting incision site.

The next program, *Smut*, marked something of a departure in proceedings, as it involved a expression generator which flashed up four words at random on the screen. Working on the assumption that eventually this process will create a statement that makes some semblance of sense—or evokes an emotional reaction of some kind—Croucher even suggests that users insert words of their own into the code in order to spice things up a bit. Following that was perhaps the most controversial mini-game of the entire collection, *Hitler*. In this scenario, the infamous genocidal totalitarian warmonger is discovered to have somehow escaped his supposed fate in the *Führerbunker* in 1945 and is now living in a nursing home in Cambridge. The player is tasked with following the elderly, wheelchair-bound dictator and placing a whoopee cushion under his position. Succeed, and Adolf will become increasingly angry. If the player can correctly guess his position on twenty separate occasions, Hitler will become so uncontrollably Führer-ous that he suffers a cardiac arrest, meaning that the game is won.

Next was *Dole*—arguably the most ambitious entry in the compilation. This political management simulator put the player into the high office of Prime Minister, and gave them a generous 1,500 days to create conditions favourable enough to cling to power. Budget cuts and monetary investment are the two options the player can choose from in order to stimulate the economy, control inflation, and keep unemployment figures as low as possible. Lose your parliamentary majority, or watch the national dole queue grow too long, and it's time for an early General Election—a poll that's unlikely to go in the incumbent's favour. (In a neat twist, as the instructions explain, the user is free to take no action at all and simply watch the country plunge into chaos.) In complete contrast, the next mini-game—*Royal Flush*—demonstrated a more monarchic theme. The action here focused on a king with a serious problem: his favourite toilet has developed a blockage somewhere beyond the royal U-bend, and he must administer just enough water from the cistern in order to clear the offending obstruction. The player can choose an amount of water ranging from 1 to 9, then must press 0 to instigate the flush. A match with the blockage's location will clear the outlet pipe and create the ideal conditions for just the right bowel movement. Underestimating the water supply will simply firm up the logjam, while an excess of cistern water will lead to a disastrous, king-sized overspill.

The penultimate mini-game was *Reagan*, in which recently-elected US President Ronald Reagan faced a quandary. Not the Cold War or the country's economic complexities, but rather the vexing need to keep his greying hair looking suitably youthful thanks to the application of his preferred hair dye, 'Greasy 2000'. To this end, the user must chase around the back of the President's head with the cursor keys, ensuring that any greying patches are immediately touched up with dye to keep up the pretence of boyish vigour. (Even the instructions jokingly point out that this is basically the exact same gameplay as demonstrated in *Acne*, but with a slightly different goal.) Rounding off the compilation in appropriately provocative style was *Ps and Qs*, in which the player is invited to guess the distance between their character and a public toilet. A value from 1 to 10 is chosen, and then the user discovers whether the flow of urine has proven to be sufficient to reach the puzzlingly transient lavatory. There are ten attempts to perfect their aim before the action resets.

*Can of Worms* hit the market for the princely sum of £3, and was supplied via mail order. The cost-effective price for a compilation proved too tempting for many early adopters of home computing to refuse, meaning that the game quickly achieved commercial success for Automata UK. While the graphics were strikingly simplistic by the standards that would soon be set by later 1980s computer systems, Croucher managed to completely subvert the expectations of his audience by producing a product that was considerably different from the simple arcade games that had previously appeared on the ZX80 and ZX81. *Can of Worms* fitted perfectly into his broader experimental ethos, which rejected mainstream gaming conventions in favour of something more cerebral and provocative. The compilation combined simple linear storytelling, cryptic messages, and unusual player interactions—elements that Croucher would refine considerably in his later work.

The title of the compilation suggests a design built around difficult choices or paradox-ical situations, as though confronting players with moral dilemmas or thought experi-ments, and this was certainly the case with entries such as *Royal Flush* and *Ps and Qs* where an element of blind luck trumped any attempt at strategic thinking even when the opposite seemed like the more obvious tactic. Yet the over-the-top satire of mini-games such as *Reagan*, or the sheer absurdity of *Hitler*, was more likely to stay in the player's mind in the long term. In a period when games were largely focused on straightforward action and elementary puzzles, *Can of Worms* stood out as an oddly intellectual challenge, foreshadowing the kind of political and philosophical discourse that later indie games would come to embrace.

While the statistical nightmare of *Dole* appeared to foreshadow other political manage-ment games such as Bug-Byte Software's *General Election* (1983), in truth the game—in a supremely tongue-in-cheek way—instead makes the point that so much of modern politics comes down to unpredictable events shaping strategy in unexpected ways, making detailed long-term planning essentially impossible. In essence, the action of the most ostensibly cerebral instalment in the collection is bound to exactly the same element of random chance as its most outlandish and scatological entries: a declaration on Croucher's part, perhaps, that real life is generally even more ridiculous than the most bizarre works of fiction, and a simple treatise not to take the world of computing—or, indeed, life itself—too seriously.

Although *Can of Worms* did not achieve mainstream critical recognition, it nonetheless remains an important artefact in the history of interactive media. Croucher's work in the early eighties very clearly paved the way for experimental storytelling in games, influencing later developers who sought to use video games as a medium for artistic and metaphysical expression. While the ZX81's technological limitations meant that *Can of Worms* was undoubtedly a simple collection of programs by modern standards, its significance lies in the compilation's overall ambition and intent rather than simply its mechanics. It serves as an example of how early computer games could be more than just recreational—they could be experimental, cheekily humorous, and even subversive.

The success of *Can of Worms* led to the release of two later games compilations from Automata UK in 1981—*Love and Death*, which presented eight new deranged mini-games on the subject of the unavoidably weighty theoretical underpinnings of the human condition, and *The Bible*: a ten-part compilation which adapted the stories of Judeo-Christian scripture in a characteristically unhinged manner. Both of these titles sold for £5, followed soon after by the later thirty game double-tape anthology *All in the Best*

*Possible Taste* (1983)—a mega-collection which must surely have been an inspiration for Cascade Games's notorious *Cassette 50* (1983) compilation.

Perhaps surprisingly, given the very basic graphical capabilities of the ZX81, these compilations landed Automata in some unexpected hot water when a Sunday tabloid ran a story accusing Croucher of selling inappropriately adult material to the fastest-growing audience for computer entertainment—namely, children. He immediately came out fighting, emphasising that the content of these mini-games was not explicit in nature, and underscoring the fact that Automata's games were always deliberately non-violent and thought-provoking. In a textbook example of no publicity being bad publicity, the debate spread to BBC Radio's *Women's Hour* and the broadsheets before eventually winding up in the House of Commons. Yet faced with Croucher's challenge to prove that any of his games had contained unsuitable adult content, none of his detractors were ever able to do so. The controversy, however, helped to ensure that the company soon became a prominent name across the UK in those seminal years of home computing.

*Can of Worms* was emblematic of Mel Croucher's unique vision: a game that defied all expectations, challenging players intellectually while also entertaining them conventionally. The reverse side of the cassette tape even contained what is thought to be the first ever stereo video game soundtrack: a true novelty in 1981, and a development which would presage further audio-visual developments from Automata UK in later years. With its experimental nature and relentlessly uncompromising wit, the compilation has become an absorbing subject for anyone interested in the early days of computer-based media experiences, and it highlights how even the earliest games could push boundaries in storytelling and engagement.

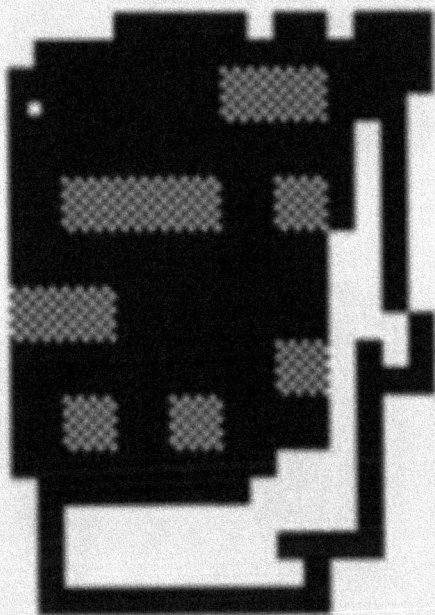

13

# ETa (1982)

Friendly aliens were all the rage in the early eighties. Thanks to the global box-office success of Steven Spielberg's *ET: The Extra-Terrestrial* (1981), audiences simply couldn't get enough of cutesy space-dwellers from other worlds, which would promptly lead to innumerable later examples of the subgenre throughout the decade including *Explorers* (Joe Dante, 1985), *Flight of the Navigator* (Randal Kleiser, 1986), and *Batteries Not Included* (Matthew Robbins, 1987), amongst many others. *ET* told the story of a diminutive member of an alien survey team who accidentally gets left behind on Earth, only to subsequently befriend a gang of human children who help him to reunite with other members of his species on a rescue mission. The film proved to be so iconic, it would become one of the most instantly recognisable cinematic tales of the 1980s.

With *ET*'s popular cultural credentials riding high, Atari infamously rushed out a tie-in game in order to release it on their Atari 2600 console in time for the lucrative Christmas retail season, hiring the well-regarded game designer Howard Scott Warshaw (creator of games such as *Yars' Revenge* and the imaginative *Raiders of the Lost Ark* adaptation) to develop the title in just five weeks. Given the heavily restricted time allotted to produce such a high-profile title, however, even a veteran designer such as Warshaw struggled to come up with the goods, meaning that Atari's *ET* adaptation wasn't just a critical and commercial failure, but became the stuff of legend as one of the most disastrously-received games of all time—and one which helped contribute to the following year's video game industry crash, given that hundreds of thousands of copies of the game were sent to landfill in Alamogordo, New Mexico following Atari's devastatingly bad fiscal year in 1983 (itself the subject of a 2014 documentary film, Zak Penn's *Atari: Game Over*).

What is less well-known, however, was that Britain had its own game which was unofficially and loosely inspired by the plot of Spielberg's masterpiece of popular cinema, and its creator was none other than a certain Mel Croucher. Released in 1982, Croucher's *ETa* was released for the 16Kb version of Sinclair's brand new ZX Spectrum computer, and is considered significant because it was one of the earliest examples of an art game (of sorts) for the platform—a form of user-centred entertainment that prioritised artistic expression over traditional gameplay mechanics. And not a flying bicycle in sight.

As was the case with other early Automata UK titles, the advertising not only trailed the plot of the game but also publicised the fact that the release came with accompanying cartoon strips and music inspired by the game. The storyline roughly followed the basic concept of the Universal Pictures blockbuster, in that a good-natured alien nicknamed 'ETa' has landed on Earth and must—with the help of the player, rather than a plucky cast of well-meaning adolescents—escape from the clutches of military scientists and make good their escape back to their home planet.

The game begins with the task of determining ETa's real name. This is not quite as straightforward a task as it may seem, as it turns out that alien names have little in common with human ones—a great deal of guesswork is required to discover the answer, and every wrong guess depletes the energy units in the alien's life support system. Just as importantly, the name is generated at random every time the game is loaded, ensuring that the same challenge remains with every replay.

Succeed in discovering your alien guest's preferred appellation, and it's on to the second level: guessing the alien's physical appearance without any visual guide. Again, the answer is different every time, adding to the longevity of the gaming experience. The guesswork here involves inputting the number of eyes, legs, and arms that the creature has—and the faster the player can hit on the right answer, the more life support units will be left for the following section.

The third level involves using the cursor keys to navigate around a maze, as the player (a humanoid figure) must track down and intercept ETa before colliding with enemies or being whisked into outer space by a constantly-moving flying saucer. (Curiously, if the creature encounters the craft on its own before the player can reach it, the game must be replayed.) Adding to the challenge is the fact that the structure of the maze is inclined to shift around, making it difficult to attempt to catch the fast-moving ETa simply by hemming the creature in. Similarly, the life support units continue to deplete at a rate of two units per second, applying a healthy measure of time pressure.

Find the errant alien in time, and then the stage is set for the concluding section: trying to reunite ETa with his interstellar spacecraft before he can be captured by a marauding guard dog. In essence, the action of this section is similar to the level which preceded it, in that the protagonist must catch up with the the alien ship while avoiding hostile non-player characters. This is easier said than done, given that by now the life support units are in perilously short supply, and the flying saucer continues to jump around randomly from one point in the maze to another. Success will largely be down to sheer good fortune if the player is to reunite his space explorer friend with the creature's landing craft so that he can return to the stars.

While the above might suggest fairly simplistic gameplay, in reality ETa stood out at the time of its release for a number of reasons. Firstly, like some of Croucher's later titles, the game introduced an element of procedurally generated gameplay. This is to say that in place of of a fixed, linear gaming experience, *ETa* generated its content dynamically—a factor which not only made each player's experience unique, but which also extended the game's lifespan by introducing an element of unpredictability to each attempt at succeeding. Not only were ETa's name and physical attributes different every time the game was played, but so too was the maze sequence a capricious experience. While the structure of the maze was given to shift (often at the least convenient time, thus heightening the tension of the time-restricted action), so too was success often predicated on factors such as where the characters and the spaceship would spawn at random.

While, like many video games of its time, *ETa* had clearly-stated objectives and win conditions, it also offered an abstract, experimental interaction. The player is invited to get to know the alien character through interaction prior to the game's central action sequence, unveiling some early AI elements in the process. *ETa* attempted to simulate, even in a modest manner, a personality that communicated with the player in unexpected ways, marking an early precursor to the kind of AI-driven experiences for which Croucher would later become recognised in his subsequent productions.

HELP I CAN'T REMEMBER MY NAME
   Press a letter to help jog my
memory. The more wrong guesses..
The shorter the time to help me.

I can only survive a short while
in the atmosphere before the 500
units in my  life-support system
are exhausted. You must be quick

                  ?????

Congratulations! Now can you
guess what WONKO looks like?

How many eyes has WONKO got?
Yes I have got 3 eyes.

How many arms have I got?
3 arms is correct. Now legs?


You've guessed what I look like
and I must look very wierd with
my 3 eyes, 3 arms and my 9 legs
but I am really very friendly!!
Press 'Z' to continue the game.



I only have 285 units left.

Croucher's trademark semantic cleverness was also in evidence with the wordplay evident in the game's title: *ETa* cheekily riffed not only on the title of Spielberg's movie, but also the notion of the titular alien's 'exact time of arrival' back on its home planet. The game subtly explored concepts like consciousness and artificial intelligence, albeit in a subtle way, predating similar metaphysical themes in later games which Croucher would become more widely known for.

Although a maze game was not by any means an obvious candidate for Croucher's signature complexity of cultural commentary, his good humour and thoughtful approach to interactive experiences were very much on display even at this early stage. Rather than presenting the kind of stereotypical bug-eyed monster typical of 1950s sci-fi B-movies, *ETa* goes to great pains to reassure the player that the eponymous character is friendly and approachable even in spite of their outlandish appearance (which, as mentioned, can differ wildly from game to game). There was something commendable about a game which celebrated difference rather than treating unfamiliar beings as hostile simply on account of their alien physiology, especially at this formative stage in computer history. *Space Invaders* this was not.

While Croucher's philosophical contemplativeness would manifest itself more clearly in later titles, *ETa* was an important precursor to those landmark games in the sense that it marked a clear evolution from his text-based Commodore PET experiences and the eccentric mini-game compilations he had created for the ZX81. The Spectrum's more colourful palette was used to create an appealing gameplay environment, with large stylised sprites and a family-friendly approach to the action. The game therefore formed an important bridge between Croucher's formative titles and the milestone experiences that were still to come.

While *ETa* was not a major commercial hit for Automata UK, likewise it was never in any danger of being consigned to the ignominy of a New Mexico landfill site, and certainly it helped in establishing Croucher's reputation as a true innovator in the gaming industry. The game had contributed to the evolution of experimental game design, and laid the groundwork for more ambitious titles in the years ahead. It was re-released the following year in a compilation alongside *Bunny* (a cheerful arcade-style game by Jason Austin) which helped to bring the game to a new audience. In spite of being heavily advertised in industry magazines such as *Popular Computing Weekly*, the game did not make much of an impact with the industry reviewers of the time. All that was to change, however, with Croucher's other release of 1982—the one which firmly put both him and Automata on the map of British computer gaming.

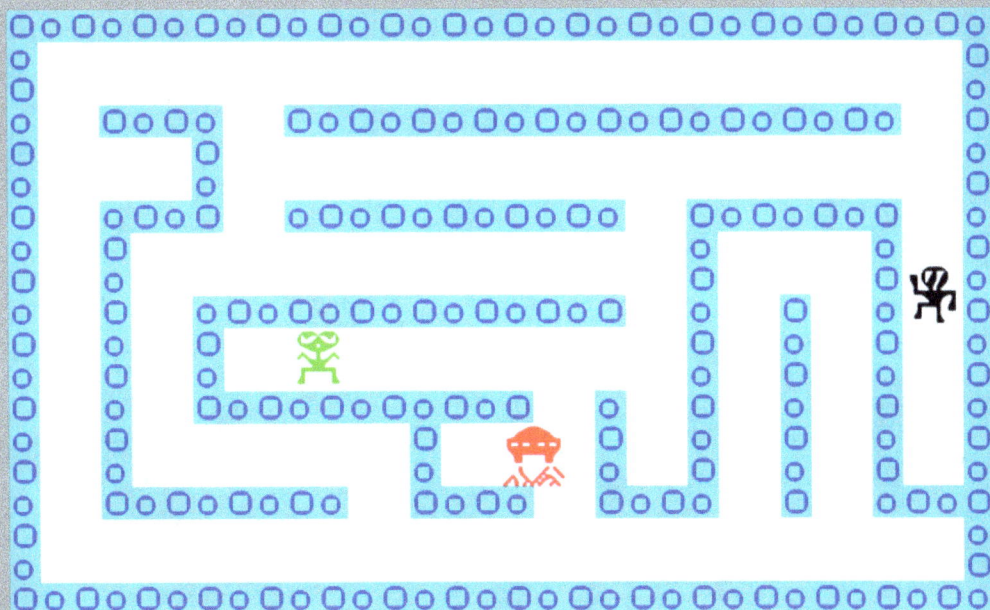

I have 324 life support units.

# PIMANIA

© Automata UK Ltd. 1982

WELCOME SEEKER, YOU STAND BEFORE
THE GATE OF π. YOUR QUEST IS TO
LOCATE THE GOLDEN SUNDIAL HIDDEN
IN TIME AND SPACE,BY THE CORRECT
INTERPRETATION OF THE TRUTH THAT
LIES WITHIN THIS PROGRAM.

ON THE APPOINTED DAY, ONE AMONG
YOU WILL BE REWARDED WITH THIS
CELEBRATED ORIGINAL TREASURE. IT
IS CRAFTED FROM GOLD,DIAMOND AND
THE RAREST OF THE EARTH'S RICHES

Press any key to begin the Quest

# PiMania (1982)

*PiMania* was one of the bravest and most significant transmedia experiments ever produced for the home microcomputer. Not only has it become known as one of the seminal Mel Croucher gaming experiences, but the fact that it was released so early in the life cycle of the Sinclair ZX Spectrum has lent the title a degree of awe and immortality that has elevated it far beyond so many of its contemporaries. Like Melbourne House's *The Hobbit* (1982), Psion's *Chess* (1982), and Ultimate Play the Game's *Jetpac* (1982), it was one of the games in the Spectrum's launch year that helped to popularise the platform and demonstrate just what the new technology was capable of.

The game was released in 1982 for the 48Kb Sinclair ZX Spectrum, the 16Kb Sinclair ZX81, the Dragon 32, and the 32Kb BBC Micro. (The ZX81 version retailed for £5, with other releases priced at the higher rate of £10 per copy.) However, it is in its Spectrum iteration that the game has become most fondly remembered. Developed by Croucher, the game typified the unconventional approach to video games taken by Automata UK, blending aspects of humour, surrealism, and multimedia elements in ways that were far ahead of their time. *PiMania* was one of the company's flagship projects, and its creative approach was heavily influenced by Croucher's background in art, music, literature, and counter-cultural thought.

The game's central concept came from Croucher's desire to blend traditional gaming with real-world interaction. He wanted to create a treasure hunt experience that extended beyond the virtual space, engaging players with cryptic puzzles and offering physical rewards as a result. In many ways, the game would take as its rough inspiration the concept behind Kit Williams' 1979 storybook *Masquerade*. Published by Jonathan Cape, that 32-page illustrated book had taken Britain by storm at the time of release, as the story included cryptic clues which eventually led two lucky winners to the hidden location of an 18-carat gold hare encrusted with jewels. (The prize was buried in the ground inside a sealed ceramic casket, partly to guard against its accidental discovery by metal detectorists but also to protect it from the elements.) It was eventually tracked down by high school physics teachers Mike Barker and John Rousseau, who correctly located the ornamental hare at Ampthill Park near Bedford. The public hysteria surrounding the search formed the basis for Bamber Gascoigne's 1983 book *Quest for the Golden Hare* (Gascoigne having acted as the celebrity witness to the hare's burial for the quest), and the huge popularity of *Masquerade* meant that it would kick off an entire 'armchair treasure hunt' genre of books.

In line with his general sense of creative ambition, however, Croucher would never have been content to simply produce a video game that attempted to emulate *Masquerade*'s success. While his early titles of the late 1970s had contained treasure hunt elements and offered clues leading to real-world prizes, *PiMania* was set to be on a different level entirely. The PiMania phenomenon would encompass not just a video game, but also a rock album; a comic strip which unfolded across Automata UK's advertising on the back page of *Popular Computing Weekly* magazine; PiMan merchandise; a magazine; a (strictly offline) social network; and—of course—the grand prize itself: a golden sundial worth £6,000 (which, taking into account inflation, would have an estimated value of £27,061 at time of writing in 2025). Yet far from allowing the 'treasure hunt' element of the game to become a mere gimmick, Croucher seemed more determined than ever that the core

Hello
I'm a
Pi Man!

gaming experience would be entertaining, thought-provoking, and even wilfully surreal. The end result would not only be a truly cross-media experience, but also one of Automata UK's most successful titles. With its eccentric but highly effective marketing techniques, including quirky newsletters and playful branding, *PiMania* soon felt less like a game and more like an offbeat cultural movement, predating the geocaching boom which would take place decades later.

*PiMania* made effective use of the limited hardware of the time to craft an engaging, graphically-illustrated text adventure. This simplicity helped the game's surreal and mysterious tone attain a level of creative prominence, but also put an inventive spin on the traditions of interactive fiction which had been established since the time of Will Crowther and Don Woods' *Colossal Cave Adventure* (1976–77). While the game retained the time-honoured 'verb noun' command style of classic text adventures, for instance, Croucher and Penfold implemented a different type of directional system: points on the compass were no longer used to indicate movement from one location to another, because numbers on an analogue clock face were now used for the same purpose. While this may have seemed like a wilfully obscure development, players would later discover that—as had been the case with so many of Croucher's games—everything had been carefully planned out for reasons which would only later become apparent to players.

On starting *PiMania*, the player is presented with a pictographic representation of 'The Gate of Pi'. Famously, many users got no further into the game than this starting screen, as they are faced with a prompt and only the cryptic instruction that 'a key turns the lock'. Hit on the right answer—the symbolic expression of pi (just the word itself won't do)—and the player is immediately cast into the domain of the PiMan: a bizarre and whimsical world, inhabited by the enigmatic humanoid character himself, bearing (as always) a $\pi$ symbol on his chest. The game presented a series of cryptic puzzles, riddles, and locations to explore, all tied to an overarching mystery: the quest for the 'Golden Sundial of Pi'—a physical treasure which was hidden in the real world.

The players was invited to navigate through the various locations of the game, solving text-based puzzles and interpreting clues. Each puzzle was intentionally opaque, requiring a fair bit of lateral thinking. The game fostered a sense of community among players who collaborated to decode its puzzles; a social aspect contributed to its longevity and legacy, only heightened by the genuine curiosity that the game generated amongst the gaming community in the trade magazines of the time.

Following a quick song-and-dance act from the PiMan to introduce the game, the player is informed that they have now moved through 'The Gate of Pi'... a notice accompanied by a brief musical burst of *My Grandfather's Clock*, presaging the game's novel method of movement between locations. The game's dreamlike graphics and accompanying music helped to create a uniquely atmospheric experience; this combination of elements was simple yet effective, given the technical limitations of the time, and certainly enhanced the enjoyment of exploring the game's twenty-one different locations.

The game also benefited from an element of randomness, along with its much-discussed sense of artificial intelligence; the PiMan could turn up at any time, and the game hinged on presenting him with an item that matched his ever-changing mood. Find the right item to suit his unpredictable disposition, and the player would be presented with a gift.

It was this selection of pi-gifts that held the key to solving the oddly otherworldly enigma that lay at the heart of the game.

*PiMania* has come to be considered a landmark title, not just for Croucher and Automata UK but for gaming history in general. The quest for the real-life Golden Sundial of Pi marked one of the earliest examples of a video game crossing over into the real world. Players had to decipher clues in the game to locate the treasure's physical location somewhere in the British Isles. This concept was revolutionary for the time, foreshadowing alternate reality games and real-world scavenger hunts in modern gaming.

While *PiMania* was highly innovative, its puzzles were notoriously cryptic, frustrating some players and limiting its audience in some circles. The game's absurdist humour and uncompromisingly offbeat style resonated with a specific subset of players in search of a challenge, but may have alienated those who were looking for more straightforward gameplay common to the time. With this in mind, the unconventional, stylised graphics and text-based interface, while charming and praised by many, might not have been as readily accessible to players who were used to more intuitive methods of game control.

It proved to be so notoriously difficult to crack the mystery at the heart of *PiMania*, many started to wonder whether the quest was actually nothing more than a convoluted joke, and became increasingly bewildered by the fact that there seemed to be no obvious punchline. In spite of this, the treasure was eventually claimed in 1985—a full three years after the game's release—which showcased not just its enduring appeal, but also the determination of the great British public to solve the treasure hunt once and for all. The worthy winners were Ilkley-based teachers Sue Cooper and Lizi Newman, who deduced that the prize could only be found on the 22nd July (given that pi is sometimes expressed as 22/7) at the Litlington White Horse on Hindover Hill near Litlington, East Sussex. So how did they succeed when so many before them had failed?

Croucher has often spoken of the sheer effort that gamers put into solving the quest, with unsuccessful treasure hunters ('PiManiacs') turning up everywhere from Stonehenge to Jerusalem in search of the PiMan's hidden sundial. For some, the quest bordered on outright obsession. So when the prize was finally won, Croucher and Penfold co-wrote a feature—'*PiMania*: The Answer'—which appeared in the October 1985 edition of *Computer & Video Games* magazine and pieced together the mind-bogglingly cryptic clues once and for all.

The game opens with 'The Gate of Pi' rising high above the ground... literally signifying 'pi in the sky'. The bewildering disco/reggae fusion *PiMania* song on the game cassette's B-side (which contained curious lyrics accompanied by the music of a Casio VL-Tone synthesizer) had numerous hints concealed within its vocals, not least 'Meet me at noon'. This motif of time continued with the game's navigational system, which (as mentioned earlier) uses the numbers on a clock face rather than compass points to move between one screen and another. The twenty-one locations on the map, when plotted out, corresponded to the stars in the constellation Pegasus—the astral horse. (Indeed, the weirdly ambiguous locations themselves lined up with the horse's anatomy: the observatory was situated where the animal's eyes would be, the cavern of ivory in place of its teeth, and so on.) Approximating the shape of this constellation would not have been possible if using standard compass directions, hence the clock-face directional system was revealed to be not just a clever innovation, but actually an essential inclusion. Once

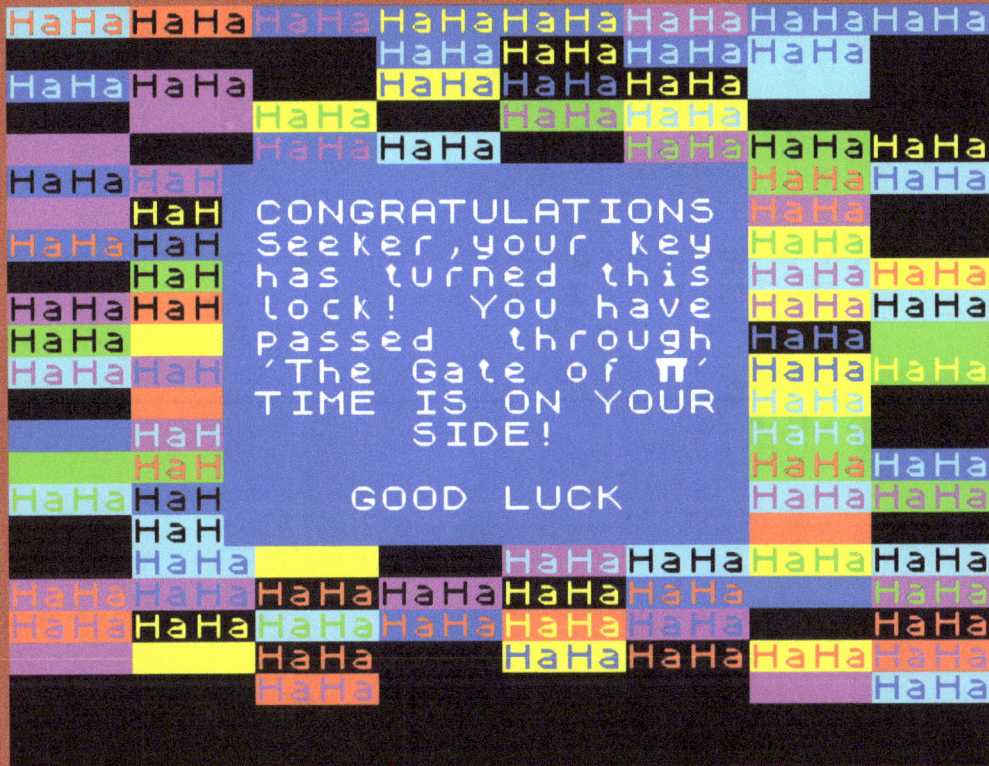

CONGRATULATIONS
Seeker,your key
has turned this
lock!  You have
passed   through
'The Gate of π'
TIME IS ON YOUR
SIDE!

GOOD  LUCK

You've fallen into a stinking waste disposal unit. You can clamber out by hitting bottom or by heading towards 9.

Pssst! Excuse me! This is the Pi Man. I'm s-scared. C-can you c-comfort m-me?

You have:
nothing
with you.

IT'S UP TO YOU TOM!
C

the PiMan had allowed the player through the green door in the game, allowing access to all of the locations, the various gifts could be used in appropriate places. While in the horse's ear (the drum), a deaf aid could be used to hear the musical notes C-A-G-G—which indicated Ca (calcium) and GG (a horse), or indeed a horse made from chalk. All of the various items gifted by the PiMan had hidden significance which could aid in the player locating the position of the sundial—some decidedly more abstruse than others (the compass related to a giant compass found near the chalk horse on Hindover Hill, for instance, while using the megaphone in the horse's mouth led to an excerpt from Psalm 33—just one chapter adjacent from Psalm 34, which is mounted on a plaque situated near to the chalk horse in Litlington. However, discerning the location was only part of the challenge: it took Cooper and Newman to make the final connection of the correct, pi-themed date and time before they arrived in the horse's mouth at noon on the 22nd of July 1985 to finally claim the prize that had eluded so many others.

With its dry humour and whimsical style, *PiMania* was an unforgettable gaming experience, and one which helped to cement the PiMan himself as cult figure in British home computing. While this was almost certainly the most infamous outing of the PiMan, it would be far from his last. The character became the mascot of Automata UK, and a more appropriate good luck charm it would be hard to conceive: he was a good-natured, surreal figure who hated profanity and abhorred violence—perfectly in line with the company's progressive, humanistic goals. The PiMan would return again and again over the next few years, with the company releasing numerous titles across several different genres (from platform action to puzzle games), many of them written by third-party programmers for publication under the Automata UK label. He even sometimes turned up in non-game software titles, such as 1985's *The PiMan's Cocktail*

*Cabinet*—a database of cocktail recipes. Between the eccentric but catchy music tracks and the character's continued appearances in the Robin Evans cartoons which accompanied Automata UK's regular advertising, the PiMan would forever be associated with the company—a fact that was aided no end by his frequent presence at public events and Microfairs.

Computer magazines of the time seemed in equal parts impressed and confused by *PiMania* and the phenomenon that accompanied it. *Your Computer*'s January 1983 issue stated 'Although we did not proceed very far with the quest, the music and graphics seemed to bear out Automata's claim that the world of the PiMan is totally bizarre'. *Personal Computer Games* seemed similarly baffled in the review for their September 1983 issue: 'The PiMan does a mean hokey-cokey. The animation makes nonsense of the fact that the Spectrum is a slow computer. And the cassette case should carry a government health warning: this game can damage your brain'. *Sinclair User* was significantly more fulsome in its praise in their January 1983 issue, noting that 'Some people may not buy the game because they think that when the competition is over the game will no longer be fun. That is not true, as it has many twists and turns before the answer is found. Locating most of them will take months. It is the best adventure game we have reviewed for the 48K Spectrum and 16K ZX81'.

With its public popularity and the intense curiosity of the trade press, *PiMania* received critical acclaim for its originality and ambition, ensuring its place in gaming history. Mel Croucher and Automata UK were among the first to emphasise creativity and artistic expression in game development over straightforward action and simplistic goals, setting an important precedent for the indie game movement that was yet to come, and *PiMania* was the clearest expression yet of Croucher's free-wheeling approach to software design. The company's rejection of corporate norms and embrace of experimentation made them a key influence on later developers, and *PiMania* has often been credited with inspiring the fusion of gaming, art, and real-world interactivity which would later be seen in titles like Niantic's *Ingress* (2013) and *Pokémon Go* (2016), Microsoft's *Minecraft Earth* (2019), and other augmented reality games. This methodology also showcased the potential for games to transcend entertainment, crafting shared cultural experiences and unleashing the player's own creativity as they sought to decipher the fiendishly obscure puzzles being offered up.

Today, Mel Croucher's *PiMania* remains a strikingly important title due to its landmark approach to digital storytelling, blending real-world elements with gaming in a way that was quite literally decades ahead of its time. Its influence can be seen in the evolution of both the augmented reality format and independent game design more generally, making it a touchstone for creativity in the gaming industry. While its cryptic nature and niche appeal may have limited its immediate impact at the time of its release, no-one can deny the national wave of interest caused by its leading-edge publicity campaign, and its soaring cultural and historical legacy is undeniable.

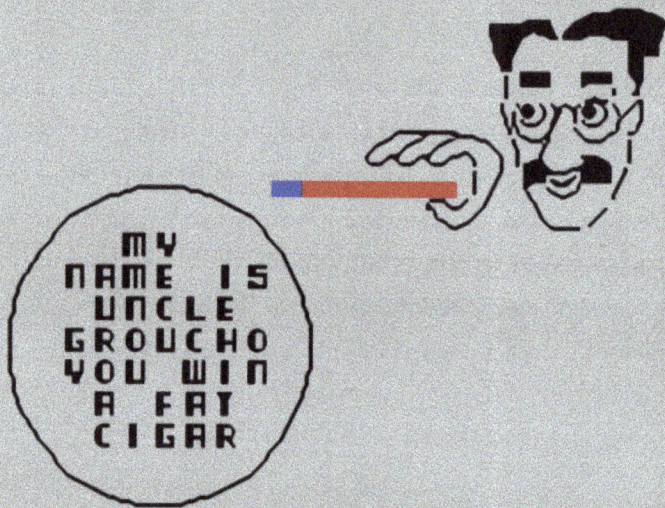

MY
NAME IS
UNCLE
GROUCHO
YOU WIN
A FAT
CIGAR

# My Name is Uncle Groucho, You Win a Fat Cigar (1983)

*My Name is Uncle Groucho, You Win a Fat Cigar* was Mel Croucher's love letter to the glorious early days of Hollywood's Golden Age—the gilded showbiz era of Buster Keaton, Clara Bow, Charlie Chaplin, Mary Pickford, and Harold Lloyd. The game is a stylistic sequel to *PiMania*, in part because it too offered an extravagantly impressive prize for the first person to solve its central puzzle, but also because the ever-present PiMan was back to once again join the action. This time around, however, the affable pink hero would be sharing the limelight with the least likely of co-stars.

Groucho Marx (1890–1977) is generally regarded as one of the finest American comedy talents in entertainment history. Initially active on stage and famous for his vaudeville routines, Marx quickly developed his fast-talking wise guy persona and became instantly recognisable due to his glasses, greasepaint moustache, cigar, and intentionally stooped posture. Later to star in many feature films between 1929 and 1968 (both in solo performances and, perhaps most famously, alongside his brothers Chico, Harpo, Gummo, and Zeppo), he successfully switched to television and radio later in his career, gaining an entirely new audience of fans thanks to his lightning-fast improvisational wit as the host of TV quiz show *You Bet Your Life*. In addition to being an actor and comedian, he was also a talented writer and singer, aiding in his reputation as one of the greatest all-round entertainers ever to grace the American film industry.

Following the commercial and critical success of *PiMania* the previous year, Automata UK sought to create an entirely new adventure game that would engage players with a brand new challenge—and a familiar, yet shrewdly different, blend of humour and puzzles. Drawing its inspiration from the cultural goldmine that was the formative years of Hollywood, the game centred around a character named Groucho who acted as a guide for players as they navigate a series of riddles and clues in order to identify famous film stars of yesteryear. Like the real Marx, this character did not suffer fools gladly, and he would be quick with a put-down if he didn't understand the wording of the player's prompts. He was also the source of an impressive range of groan-inducingly corny gags sprinkled liberally throughout the game.

The game's title did more than simply reflect its whimsical nature, as 'You Win a Fat Cigar' didn't just allude to Groucho Marx's iconic prop. In the game, the player starts with a total of 200 cigars, and will quickly find that their supply is depleted if they need to trade for purchases, procure clues to puzzles, or encounter the PiMan who will invariably ask to 'borrow' a few (thus mirroring his tendency to pilfer objects at random throughout the proceedings of *PiMania*). Thankfully Groucho's stock of cigars can be replenished as the game continues, perhaps by some good fortune at gambling or in the process of answering questions correctly, and the show can go on.

With a reminder that Hollywood is the land where anything can happen (and frequently does), and a quick burst of Irving Berlin's *There's No Business Like Showbusiness* (1946), the player is promptly thrust into the United States of the inter-War years... where, in much the same manner as the game's predecessor, pi is the key that gets the action moving. Like *PiMania* before it, Groucho is no straightforward text adventure game.

(Indeed, entering traditional interactive fiction commands will meet with a cheeky reminder that this is no Scott Adams title—referring to the famous game designer who founded Adventure International in 1979.) Instead, it's left up to the player to discern which commands will get them closer to their goal of uncovering Groucho's riddles—the answers to which will tend to hearken back to the often-obscure giants of the acting world between the 1920s and '50s. Get it wrong, and expect an acid-tongued jibe from a deeply unimpressed (and endlessly sarcastic) Mr Marx.

Players could navigate between different locations in each area, with different gameplay opportunities being offered by the places they visit. There's a bar where clues rather than drinks are on sale, while the casino gives visitors the chance to try their luck at a roulette wheel—though as in real life, the house seldom loses. A trip to the bank, on the other hand, reveals the surprising fact that cigars rather than dollars are the favoured currency… and depending on the available supply at any given time, applying for a loan might just be a necessary evil to keep the player's investigations moving forward. There are, naturally, surprises to be encountered where least expected, and—in keeping with the game's cinematic theme—nothing is ever quite as it initially seems.

The game was a deeply quirky text adventure title with some role-playing elements, augmented by stylised graphics, where players must interact with Groucho (who pops up randomly to accompany the action—often in some unanticipated places) in order to receive clues about the identity of the aforementioned famous, but usually rather abstruse, range of film stars. Upon guessing correctly, players receive another clue which will lead them to a different star, and so on. The puzzles were scattered over five different playing areas across America: Metroville, Tinsel Town, Burger Valley, Injun Creek, and

Wrinkle City. Only if the player is successful in uncovering all 22 of the clues to the identity of one very particular movie legend would they have all the information they would need to solve the key puzzle that lay behind the game.

The game was surprisingly atmospheric, in spite of its graphics not exactly being photo-realistic in nature, and with so many big stars of yesteryear being in the spotlight as the game continues, it was easy to get swept up into Groucho's world—a strangely non-specific land of vintage twentieth century Americana which seemed to effortlessly straddle several decades of the entertainment industry in one go. *Uncle Groucho* certainly managed to evoke some element of the crazy, unpredictable, and frequently improvisational environment of unregulated pre-Hays Code Hollywood, and with a pithy wit of which the real Marx would surely have approved. This particular historical setting, with its 'anything goes' ethos, allowed for a welcome element of randomness in the now-expected Croucher style. Yet what really made the game memorable, of course, is the endless stream of one-liners, puns, and eye-wateringly excruciating jokes that brought the spirit of Groucho alive throughout proceedings.

Like its predecessor, *My Name is Uncle Groucho* famously incorporated a competition element. Mirroring the success of *PiMania*, the prize was suitably extravagant to garner considerable interest from the industry press—and as Croucher was at pains to explain in subsequent media interviews, significant effort was also put into ensuring that the challenge this time would not prove to be quite so insurmountable. Players who correctly identified the mystery film star were invited to post their answers to the company, entering a prize draw that was held on the 1st of June 1984. The first prize was a trip to Hollywood on Concorde to meet the identified famous actor, with a return trip on the

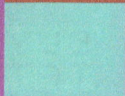   

Hi there! Nice to meet you buddy
Guess who I am tonight.Each clue
costs you 2©s more than the last
Max:10 clues. The first is FREE.

luxury cruise liner *QE2*. The competition was eventually won by Phil Daley of Stoke on Trent, who correctly identified Mickey Mouse as the mystery public figure, and provided the (now infamous) winning pun: 'There's no blood in our games, it's all tomata sauce.'

In addition to the game's success with players—certainly not hampered by the prospect of the epic prize awaiting the lucky winner, which was trailed prominently by the media—*Uncle Groucho* was also a persona that would be gleefully embraced by Croucher himself in public appearances. He even appeared in character on Central Independent Television's short-lived computer-themed magazine show *Magic Micro Mission* in 1983, alongside the PiMan, where 'Groucho' triumphantly bamboozled presenters Adrian Hedley and Jo Wheeler with the kind of trademark instantaneous wit that would have impressed the late Marx himself. Dressed in the character's trademark frock coat and top hat, waving his cigar around for all he was worth, the appearance not only gave Croucher the opportunity to promote the game but also to reinforce Automata's wider mission to provide non-violent, thought-provoking, intentionally ridiculous entertainment for players of all ages—a sentiment which no doubt went down well with the programme's youthful audience at the time. Charismatic as ever, Croucher's appearances on TV helped to confirm his status as a truly medium-transcendent personality, ensuring that his professional reputation transcended that of many of his contemporaries in game design.

Keith Campbell stated in the January 1984 issue of *Computer & Video Games* that 'the format of *Groucho* is different from that of *PiMania*, and comes across as a series of zany puzzles and joky insults, interspersed with tunes and set against a background of clever and colourful animated pictures. [...] *Groucho* is entertaining and addictive enough to be played again and again.' *Popular Computing Weekly*'s 27th October 1983 edition was also effusive in its admiration, noting that 'a quick play suggests that *Groucho* is well up to *PiMania* standard and is full of the dubious programming, great jokes and ideas that made *PiMania* such a winner.' Graham Taylor of *Micro Adventurer* was similarly impressed in their December 1983 issue, noting that: '*My Name is Uncle Groucho, You Win a Fat Cigar* maintains Automata's reputation as leaders of the *Monty Python* school of programming. [...] An excellent game Pimaniacs and those yet to be converted will love. The free hit single on the reverse of the cassette is wonderful.'

In true Automata style, *My Name Is Uncle Groucho, You Win a Fat Cigar* was noteworthy for its imaginative integration of gameplay with real-world rewards: a concept that was still in its infancy at the time, and which ensured that Croucher received deserved recognition for the evolution of a hybrid game format that he had been championing since the late 1970s. The game's blend of witty humour, celebrity culture, and unorthodox storytelling reflected Croucher's creative vision, and helped to explain just why he continues to be celebrated as a true innovator in the British video game industry.

While *Uncle Groucho* may not have achieved the same level of fame as some of Croucher's other titles, it was still a high-profile release for Automata UK, and remains a testament to the experimental and whimsical nature of early 1980s video game development. Its highly distinctive approach to player engagement, and the incorporation of an extensively reported real-world competition, highlighted a unique creative period in gaming history, showcasing the potential of games to extend beyond the screen and interact with players' lives in meaningful ways—something that Croucher has always excelled at.

CHEAP-WINES WHISKEY COLD-BEERS

RICKY'S
BAR

KNOCK! KNOCK!    WHO'S THERE?
MARTINI
MARTINI WHO?
MARTINI HANDS ARE FROZEN!

# dEuS EX MACHINA

DO NOT SWITCH OFF YOUR COMPUTER!
THIS PROGRAM WILL BE NEEDED WHEN
LOADING SIDE TWO. PRESS 'S' KEY.

# Deus Ex Machina (1984)

Now immortalised in gaming history, *Deus Ex Machina* wasn't just Automata UK's crowning glory—it was, in fact, one of the single most ambitious digital experiences of the 1980s. It seems almost discourteous to consider it solely as a game, for *Deus Ex Machina* offered users a truly immersive multimedia event which—in a very real sense—almost made this cassette-loaded program feel like a CD-ROM-style experience that had arrived a decade too early. The result was a release which has not only become one of the most heavily-analysed pieces of software of the 1980s, but also a title which continues to be discussed in computer game design courses even today.

It is difficult to overstate the sheer aspiration of *Deus Ex Machina*, and it has subsequently become widely regarded as a pioneering title in the history of video games. Released in 1984 for platforms like the ZX Spectrum, Commodore 64, and MSX, it was developed over a number of years by Croucher—who, famously, put so much faith in the project, he committed his life savings to bringing it to life. The staggering clarity of his artistic vision remains tangible throughout. The game broke away from conventional gaming norms of the time, introducing an experimental cross-media experience that aimed to elevate video games to the level of a true artistic medium. Unlike most games of the same era, which primarily focused on reflex-based gameplay and a rigidly linear storyline, *Deus Ex Machina* instead sought to convey an original narrative which was affected by the user's choices. Blending philosophical themes with a surreal, immersive audio-visual experience, it was a bold experiment that attempted to fuse gaming, music, and storytelling in a way that had never been done before.

The game's conception was profoundly tied to Croucher's counter-cultural ideals; it built upon his and the Automata UK team's willingness to experiment with merging computer gameplay with other forms of art, creating new forms of media engagement. Automata had, by now, already firmly established itself as an unorthodox game studio, always prioritising creativity over profitability and emphasising a human quality to gaming that was inevitably lacking in the more conventional fare of the time. While Croucher was very much the driving conceptual force behind *Deus Ex Machina*, credited as its writer and director (and responsible for its elaborate sense of cinematic verve), the coding responsibilities for the game fell to Andrew Stagg for the famous ZX Spectrum version, with Colin Jones adapting the title for the MSX and Commodore 64.

Croucher envisioned a user-focused experience that combined visuals, sound, and narrative, leading to the decision to package the game's data cassette with a separate audio cassette. This derived from Croucher's bold prediction that by the mid-eighties, games would start to include celebrity performances, hence his determination to get ahead of his competitors. (In reality, it demonstrated once again his tendency to foresee the market far in advance; while there would be countless film and TV tie-ins during the age of the home micros, the arrival of actual actors in computer games *en masse* wouldn't occur until the full motion video boom of the CD-ROM era from the mid-nineties onwards.) The audio cassette contained a fully synchronised soundtrack and narration to accompany the gameplay, featuring dialogue delivered by a number of notable performers of the time such as the velvet-voiced Jon Pertwee (famous as BBC TV's third incarnation of *Doctor Who* and affable scarecrow *Worzel Gummidge*, as well as on radio in *The Navy Lark*), Frankie Howerd (whose famous *double-entendres* had made him an instantly-recognisable comic talent on British stage and screen from the 1950s onwards, including in many *Carry On* films), and Ian Dury (the post-punk/new wave era rock singer who was the vocalist and lyricist of bands Kilburn and the High Roads and Ian Dury and the Blockheads). Rounding up this unique line-up of performance talent was singer Donna Bailey, historian and peace campaigner E.P. Thompson (as 'The Voice of Reason'), and Croucher himself—who, in addition to delivering distinctive vocals, also composed and performed an entire original soundtrack for the game. Not only was this approach entirely cutting-edge for a home micro release, but it also circumvented the limitations of the systems' constrained audio capabilities of the time, supplanting chiptunes with a truly unique instrumental playlist. Between its line-up of celebrity involvement and its otherworldly musical soundscape, *Deus Ex Machina* was, quite literally, unlike anything that had ever been attempted before.

With a polymathic knowledge of the arts, Croucher drew inspiration from a variety of different sources for *Deus Ex Machina* which included classical literature, live theatre, and music. The game's title—Latin for 'God from the Machine'—alludes to the theatrical concept of an unexpected power suddenly resolving conflicts. This could be an improbable or even contrived event that suddenly provides the answer to a seemingly unsolvable problem in a story, thus reflective of the game's theme of the cycle of creation, decay, and renewal. In turn, it also riffed on *Hamlet*, Act 2, Scene 2, where the eponymous Prince of Denmark famously remarks: 'What a piece of work is man! How noble in reason! How infinite in faculty! In form and moving how express and admirable! In action how like an angel! In apprehension how like a god! The beauty of the world! The paragon of animals! And yet, to me, what is this quintessence of dust?' Just as Hamlet perceived the potential grandeur of humanity and its works, he ultimately perceived it as empty and futile without purpose, again echoing the game's key themes surrounding the human condition. The narrative of *Deus Ex Machina* also took cues from *Brave New World* by Aldous Huxley and several other dystopian literary works of the twentieth century, not least of them George Orwell's *Nineteen Eighty-Four*, focusing on humanity's technological overreach and its inevitable impact on the natural rhythm of life.

The true essence of the game lay not with a rigid story, but rather with the grandest of concepts: the nature of human life itself. Croucher offered the player the chance to take a nascent entity from the point of conception and then guide and shape it through every stage of development. To do this, he would hearken back to one of literature's most powerful evocations of personal development. William Shakespeare's phrase 'All the world's a stage' comes from his play *As You Like It*, Act 2, Scene 7, and is the opening line of a monologue in which Shakespeare compares life to a theatrical performance, where people are merely actors playing different roles throughout their lives: 'All the world's a stage,/And all the men and women merely players;/They have their exits and their entrances,/And one man in his time plays many parts,/His acts being seven ages.' As the dialogue suggests, this leads us to the Bard's famous concept of the Seven Ages of Man—each of them representing the different stages a person goes through: The Infant (helpless and dependent); the Schoolboy (querulous and reluctant); the Lover (passionate and emotional); the Soldier (ambitious and seeking honour); Justice (the wisdom and respect of middle age); Old Age (weak and in decline); and the Second Childhood (losing faculties in extreme old age and returning to a state of dependence).

The actual gameplay of *Deus Ex Machina* was highly unconventional. Trying to describe it as a series of mini-games would be akin to describing the *Mona Lisa* as a series of reasonably skilful brush-strokes. The narrative revolved around the journey of a

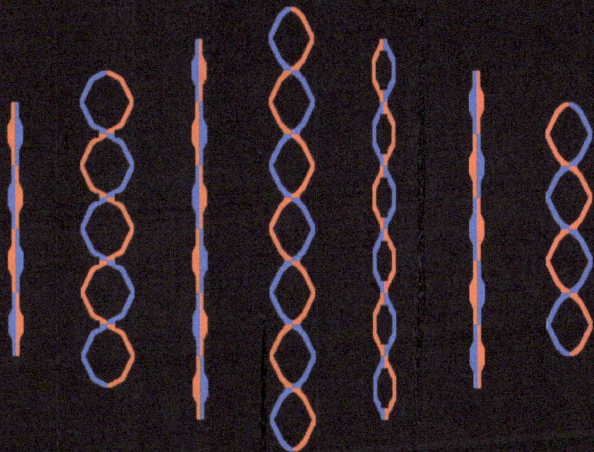

THE
D.N.A.
WELDER

DEGREE
OF
IDEAL-
ENTITY
??%

EEG

ECG

THE INCUB-ATOR

DEGREE OF IDEAL-ENTITY 76%

EEG

ECG

'defective' being through the stages of its life: conception, birth, childhood, adulthood, and death. (A 'defective' individual, we come to understand, refers here to a unique human being who has somehow managed to escape both society's and the Machine's idea of efficient uniformity.) Due to its ambitious nature, the game required twice the amount of memory being offered by the 48Kb Spectrum at the time, meaning that two separate loads were required in order to access all of the data. Once the user had played through the first collection of sections, their progress would be recorded and then the second load took place—an early example of a multi-load title; a practice which would become commonplace later in the decade. In a laudable addition, *Deus Ex Machina* was also packaged with a complete transcript of all in-game dialogue so that any users with hearing impairments would not feel excluded from the action in any way.

In the grand tradition of cinematic events, there is a star at the heart of proceedings of *Deus Ex Machina*—in this case, the player themselves. The whole single-player multimedia experience takes around fifty minutes to complete, with the knowledge that it can be replayed over and over again while yielding slightly different results every time. Just as there is no way to conventionally 'win,' so too is it impossible to 'lose'. As the game's instructions explain, between 1987 and 1994, the information systems of the UK gradually become integrated into a single, centralised computer data bank—a vast Machine that came to govern every aspect of the country's defence and internal organisation. But what if the Machine had to suddenly face a challenge of an unexpected nature: one that couldn't be anticipated even by its vast wealth of data?

The action begins with the news that the last mouse on Earth has just died, having taken refuge inside The Machine, and its terminal dropping has had a decidedly unexpected impact on the workings of the contraption's rusting innards. The player must, at all costs, protect this genetic material from the observation of the Machine. They are thus invited to take control of the DNA Welder, using coloured blocks to impact on the behaviour and character of several DNA double helices by keeping them spinning. They must also avoid a blue block—the Defect Police scanner—which seeks to pinpoint anomalies in the system. An onscreen display indicates the 'degree of ideal-entity': a figure which depletes in line with the amount of uniqueness that the character loses as the game progresses. Should this meter hit zero, the protagonist will assume the mundane quality of being just like any other run-of-the-mill human being in society.

Next, the Cell Producer calls on the player to keep a series of cells pulsating by gently agitating them, while still avoiding the fast-moving blue scanner of the Defect Police. Similar action governs the following stage, The Memory Bank, where the user must keep the memories in motion while continuing to evade the ever-present scanner. The cells are starting to take a more structured form by the time of the next level, the Belle Bank, and then the following section—the Beau Bank—involves players colliding their cursors with sperm in order to divert their path and fertilise a human egg. (This is accompanied by Ian Dury's marvellously gravelly vocals as he intones 'I'm a fertilising agent.') By the time of the Incubator, the user must keep the now-fully-developed foetus safe within a barrier of cells while still evading the Defect Police's ever-watchful scanner.

The Umbilicus sees the hapless baby ejected from the incubator and unwittingly thrust into the strange and unforgiving world beyond its confines. It's up to the player to guide this tiny infant by spinning it away from the ever-present eyes of the Defect Police (not an easy task, as their agents are everywhere). The Interrogation Tank adds a different dimension to this task; the entity, now a more mature youth, must be protected from scans from surrounding Defect Police cameras. Fail to provide adequate cover and the 'degree of ideal-entity' will decrease as it is exposed to greater scrutiny from the authorities (voiced by the unforgettable Frankie Howerd).

The player is invited to turn over the cassette for the second half of the game, which contains the adult life cycle of the protagonist. In The Soldier, the grown human jogs from left to right while bombarded by obstructions from all sides. A three-part shield, which covers the figure's front, back, and head, can be adjusted to fend off these unwanted projectiles. Survive that, and the user will reach The Justice. Here, the perspective changes so that the entity—now in middle age—must shamble somewhat lethargically towards the screen, faced with the prospect of trampling negative concepts while safely jumping over the positive ones. This allows them to retain 'peace' and 'good' at the same time as decimating 'war' and 'evil'. Careful timing is necessary, however— especially if the player wants to avoid the length of rusty barbed wire in their path which has a tendency to appear when least convenient.

The final level, Second Childishness, witnesses the rather melancholic process of trying to keep the now-elderly being alive by preventing blot clots. This is achieved through a return to the kind of action that typified the beginning of the game, with subsections such as Blood Clot Dispersal, White Cell Deterioration, and Red Cell Shepherding. However, as in all lives, this is simply a case of delaying the inevitable, and eventually even the player's best efforts will see their character's life come to an end. However, as the soundtrack explains, the cycle of life is unending... and what if we realised that this whole experience was all simply one big digital simulation, where we could replay the events of our life in detail over and over again until we got the conclusion that we most desired?

Even now, *Deus Ex Machina* is lauded for the skill of its visual aspects; while they may seem outwardly simplistic today due to the hardware limitations of the time, in reality they were abstract, symbolic, and superbly animated, representing the various stages of life with a surreal, dreamlike quality that was never to be truly replicated by any other title on the home micros. The gameplay was not intended to be overly challenging or competitive. Instead, it served more as an interactive conceptual accompaniment to the soundtrack than it did as an end unto itself. The careful synchronisation of the visuals and audio—as mentioned earlier—was a core part of the experience, with players instructed to play the cassette and game simultaneously. This approach further emphasised the fact that the game was less of a traditional computer game and more of an experiential event, with the dialogue of the actors seamlessly interwoven into the mesmerising musical numbers and onscreen action. As the narrator, Jon Pertwee added significant gravitas to the surreal and often humorous script with his instantly-recognisable stentorian tones, and the game benefits hugely from the involvement of unique performers such as Ian Dury, Frankie Howerd, and Professor E.P. Thompson, further enhancing the emotional resonance of the experience. The musical soundtrack, which was so integral to the game's storytelling, guided players skilfully through the emotional beats of the story, turning the overall experience into an audio-visual symphony the likes of which only Croucher could have created.

*Deus Ex Machina* proved to be deeply contemplative, exploring many themes such as free will, the role of technology, individuality, and the cyclical nature of life. The game

DEFECT POLICE INTERROGATION TANK

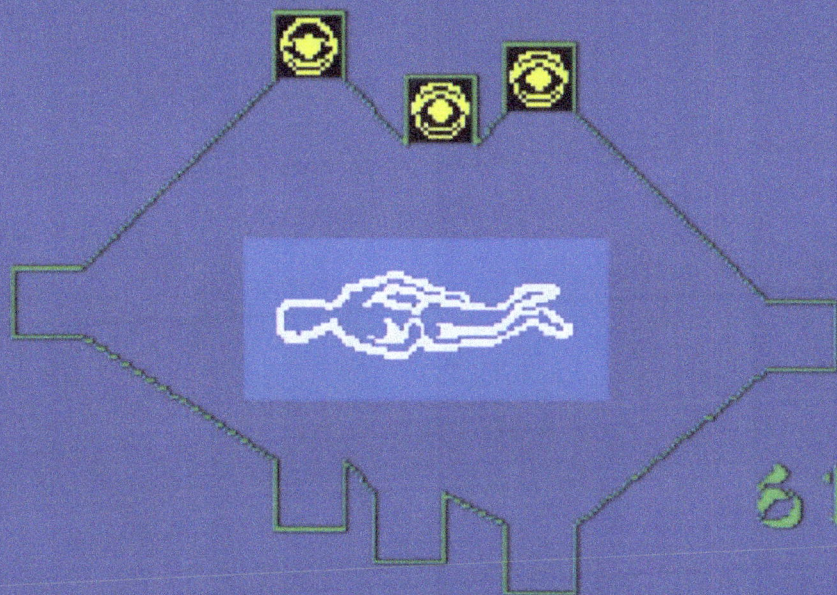

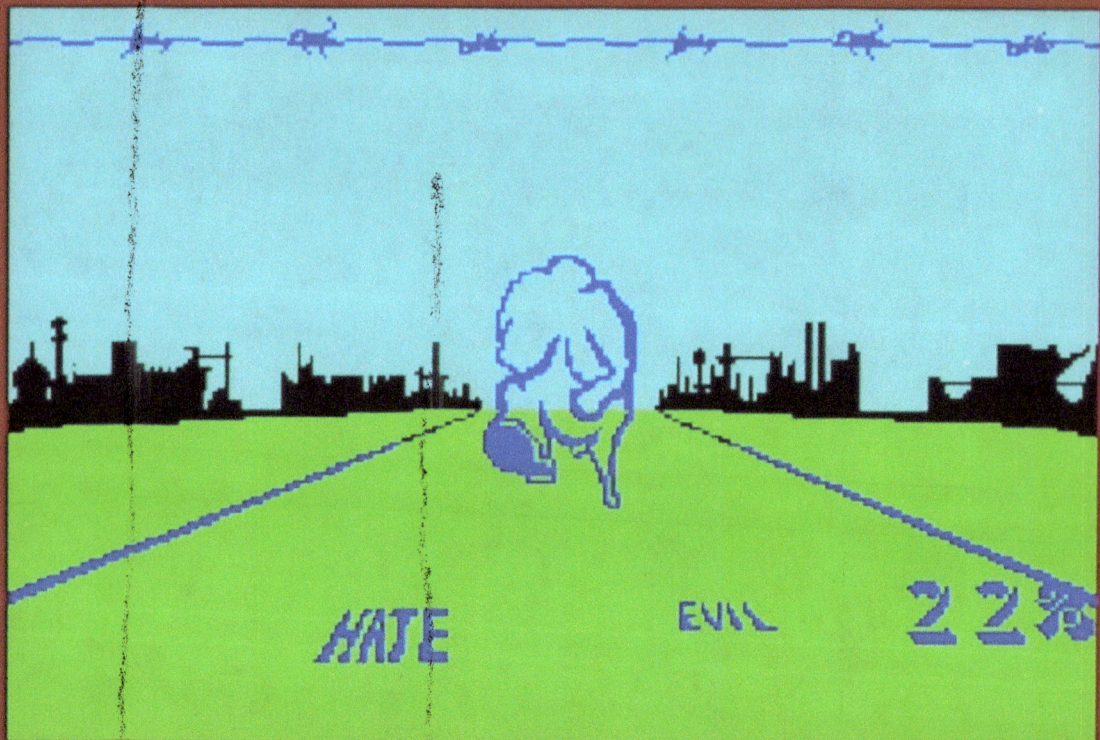

was critical of the growing mechanisation of society, reflecting Croucher's concerns about the potentially dehumanising effects of modern technology. While he was always keen to harness the capacity of computers for good—as a medium for creative expression and socio-cultural commentary—he was similarly never unaware of the likelihood of the problems that could be caused by technology if abused or taken to excess. With the Machine, we witness a digital entity capable of acting like a god, seemingly benign in and of itself and yet potentially capable of terrifying levels of control over the populace it was designed to serve. Several of Croucher's earlier, anarchic titles had made clear his depth of concern surrounding authoritarianism in all its forms, and never was the point made more succinctly that tyranny is no more nor less palatable whether its origins derive from carbon or silicon. Yet ultimately, the ethos of *Deus Ex Machina* remains a positive one; it would be easy to interpret a game where every strategy ultimately ends in the protagonist's death to be somewhat bleak and fatalistic, and yet in reality the opposite is true. The game, instead, has an emphasis on the endless universal cycle of rebirth and renewal that pointed more towards Far Eastern mysticism than it ever did to the totalitarian warnings of Huxley and Orwell, with a sense of hopeful optimism that underpinned its repeatable playability.

Determined to ensure that this larger-than-life experience received the release it deserved, Croucher opted for a 'big box presentation'—luxurious, laminated packaging which made the game instantly memorable, but also added somewhat to its retail price of £14.99. As well as containing the all-important two cassette tapes, the game also came bundled with a poster of the game's striking cover artwork, further enhancing its sense of cinematic gloss. While many later games for the home micros of the 1980s would feature premium packaging like this, at the time of release it seemed like a genuinely noteworthy innovation; one which was only further underscored when high street retailer WH Smith complained that due to the boxes' unusual size, individual branches were unable to fit them into the standardised retail shelving which had been designed for smaller plastic single- and double-cassette cases. (Automata UK would instead fall back on their tried and tested strategy of mail order sales when it came to retailing the game.) The classiness of the physical production, therefore, only heightened *Deus Ex Machina*'s reputation for sophisticated refinement.

At the time of its release, *Deus Ex Machina* divided computer industry reviewers. Some critics praised the game's ambition and artistic vision, while others criticised its unconventional gameplay and lack of clear score-driven goals. Many players struggled to categorise the title at all, given the extent to which it had defied traditional gaming norms. A few, for instance, raised a note of concern that as the onscreen action was strictly curtailed by the synchronised narrative of the audio cassette, some of the mini-games seemed to be essentially rushed in order to fit them into the tightly-packed time confines of the meticulously-planned audio-visual playing experience. In the main, however, the reception of commentators was one of respect and appreciation, given how many had been genuinely impressed by the game's scope and innovation. '*Deus Ex Machina* is a noble development idea, which points towards a new understanding of what can be done with computer games,' noted Robin Candy and Roger Kean in *Crash* magazine's November 1984 issue. *Home Computing Weekly* was similarly effusive in its appraisal of the game's merits when their review appeared in the 23rd October 1984 edition: 'To call this a game is an insult. It's a stunning and profound audio-visual experience. [...] This epic plot takes one hour to unfold. Is "value for money" a meaningful concept in the face of something unique? Don't fail to see this.' John Gilbert of *Spectrum User* joined the chorus of approval in their magazine's December 1984 issue: 'Croucher has cleverly manipulated the elements of computer gaming and brought in concepts usually found only in movies. The result is a piece of software which even those people who usually find games boring and computers even more so, will enjoy and play time and again.' Even the more sceptical reviews tended more towards befuddlement than negativity, with the most frequent criticisms being the game's high retail price point for the time, and the finicky practice of keeping the game and music cassettes perfectly synchronised.

Commercially, the game did not perform as well as had been hoped, as the niche public appeal of its alternative approach and the high retail price point of the release ultimately limited its audience—though it did break even in the end. The game eventually achieved a cult reputation, but ironically this heightened popularity as an underground sleeper hit led to it being widely pirated both at home and across Europe. Perhaps most troublingly of all, due to the ground-breaking nature of having two tapes essential to the game's action rather than the usual one, most pirate groups only duplicated the program cassette with no attempt to recreate the accompanying audio cassette. This led to considerable puzzlement for those who would eventually play the game in this way, as it appeared to be a completely silent experience with no explanation about what was actually supposed to be happening (and unlike the commercial release, there wasn't even a printed transcript to fall back on). Bereft of its musical accompaniment and dialogue performances, pirated versions led to little more than a pale shadow of Croucher's intended multimedia odyssey. Yet despite these setbacks, *Deus Ex Machina* still earned a solid following amongst its many fans, and was widely lauded for pushing the boundaries of what computer games could ultimately be.

*Deus Ex Machina* was the winner of Game of the Year at the Computer Trade Association Awards in 1985, and was runner-up for *Computer & Video Games* magazine's much sought-after Golden Joystick Award for Best Original Game of the Year in 1984 (losing out only to David Braben and Ian Bell's legendary space trading game, *Elite*), underscoring industry recognition for Croucher's efforts to delineate new limits of what was possible with home computer titles. Not only did its cerebral nature mark a very clear departure from the video arcade-dominated style of action title that had dwarfed computer gaming until this point, but it has since become recognised as a clear precursor to the 'art games' movement, influencing later titles that sought to blend narrative, emotion, and gameplay in inventive ways. Today, *Deus Ex Machina* is celebrated as one of the first games to truly challenge the notion of video games as mere entertainment, presenting them as a medium for artistic expression as much as conventional controller-driven action. It would eventually pave the way, decades later, for diverse titles such as Playdead's *Limbo* (2010); The Chinese Room's *Everybody's Gone to the Rapture* (2015); Thatgamecompany's *Journey* (2012); and Giant Sparrow's *What Remains of Edith Finch* (2017), all of which place emphasis on narrative and emotion rather than strictly focusing on game mechanics. *Deus Ex Machina*'s extensive use of synchronised audio tracks, incorporating dialogue and music, was well ahead of its time, prefiguring many later experiments in user-focused storytelling which would include rhythm-based narratives.

*Deus Ex Machina* was an experience that truly broke the mould, challenging the boundaries of gaming as a digital art form while still providing eminently playable entertainment. Its experimental nature and philosophical themes set it far apart from its peers, making it a landmark in video game history and laying the groundwork for later, boldly conceptual titles such as Denton Designs' *Frankie Goes to Hollywood* (1985)

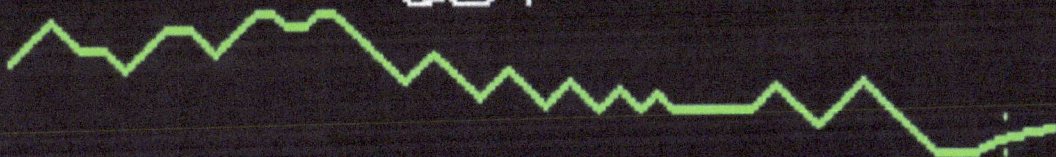

for Ocean Software, and the CRL Group's *The Rocky Horror Show* (1985). While it was not a resounding commercial success, the legacy of *Deus Ex Machina* endures as a strident creative statement about the artistic potential of video games. Its critical legacy cannot be overstated, for the game's sheer ambition inspired countless developers to investigate the potential of unconventional storytelling and cross-media integration in their games.

Such was Croucher's commitment to the *Deus Ex Machina* concept, he has revisited the title numerous times over the years. These have included a re-release via Electric Dreams in 1986, which brought the title to the attention of an entirely new range of players, and—several decades later—Croucher would return to the concept afresh with *Deus Ex Machina 2* in 2015, this time featuring legendary actor Sir Christopher Lee as the narrator alongside a new cast of talented performers. This sequel/remake was to make the most of the vast leap in technological capabilities that had occurred in computer systems since the 8-bit micros which had been host to the original game. But that development will be explored in more detail later in this book.

Automata UK's work remains a testament to the power of creativity and vision in an industry often dominated by commercial considerations, and *Deus Ex Machina* was arguably the company's greatest and most visible achievement. Yet in a bittersweet turn of events, the game was also to become famous as one of the last that the business would ever produce. By 1985, dismayed by *Deus Ex Machina*'s commercial under-performance and disillusioned with the general direction of the British computer game industry, Croucher decided—after much consideration—to exit the market. As he discussed in numerous interviews both at the time and in later years, Croucher was highly suspicious of the encroaching commercialisation of the industry, which he felt was leading to an inevitable focus on profitability and marketability at the expense of creative endeavour and artistic innovation. He knew that this aggressively commercially-driven direction could never be reconciled with the Automata UK vision of using software development—and multimedia strategies more widely—as a form of artistic empowerment and cultural expression. His decision to sell the company to his long-time friend and business partner Christian Penfold, therefore, was motivated by a principled desire to end the Automata dream while it still had integrity and evoked so many positive memories amongst those who had played their games over the years. (As it happened, Penfold dissolved the company only a few months later, ensuring that the ethical culture championed by Croucher and himself would remain forever unsullied by the relentless march of corporatisation.) While Croucher may have believed that this development would mark the end of his involvement with the still-nascent computer game industry, however, it transpired that fate would have other ideas.

WRITTEN BY
MEL CROUCHER
&
COLIN JONES

# iD (1986)

With the Automata UK years now behind him, it seems important to note that Croucher was not only lauded throughout the games industry for his work as the creative force behind games such as *PiMania* and *Deus Ex Machina*—he had been, directly or indirectly, responsible for the release of around 65 software titles by the company, many of them giving a voice to brand new game designers for the first time. His ethos of non-violence resonated far and wide, especially in an industry which had become dominated by unadventurous arcade action, and there was curiosity about if and how his involvement with computer games would continue following his departure from Automata.

The answer came in the form of *iD*: a very different type of game, and one that came from an unexpected origin. Clement Chambers, the charismatic owner of the CRL Group, negotiated with Croucher to bring a brand new kind of gaming experience to the home micros; one which was altogether more cerebral and unpredictable than that which had come before. Under Chambers' leadership, the CRL Group (originally named 'Computer Rentals Ltd.', from the days when the company leased out computer equipment) was responsible for some of the best and most unapologetically original games ever to reach home microcomputers. These included Pete Cooke's sprawling planetary exploration simulator *Tau Ceti* (1985) and its world-hopping sequel *Academy* (1986); Rod Pike's controversial horror text adventure *Dracula* (1985) and its follow-ups; satirical time travel arcade adventure *Doctor What!* (1986), and countless others. By midway through the eighties, Chambers was looking to diversify his company's range still further, and plans were announced for a new label—'Nu-Wave'—which would showcase the company's more experimental and *avant garde* titles. In particular, Chambers was especially eager to spotlight a gaming experience which featured artificial intelligence at its core—an area of great interest in 1980s pop culture, not least thanks to films such as *WarGames* (John Badham, 1983) and *Electric Dreams* (Steve Barron, 1984).

While Croucher's time with Automata UK may have been over by 1986, he remained just as committed to ambitious plans for the future of home computing. As always, he saw the market as infinitely more than an endless sea of arcade conversions for high-score enthusiasts, and perceived the home micros as an invaluable medium for making profound socio-cultural points in a way that players would find actively engaging rather than passively presented. To this end, with *iD* he was to produce an experience that was quite different from *Deus Ex Machina*; it became his aim to create a game where the nature of the players' input would significantly influence the narrative outcome. Working with programmer Colin Jones, Croucher envisioned an experience that would reflect aspects of the player's own unique personality, encouraging introspection and self-discovery rather than pushing the action in the direction of a pre-existing narrative trajectory.

While *iD* was an interactive fiction experience, it abandoned any pretence of a conventional text adventure parser in favour of a chatbot-style approach. While a chatbot interface (an application designed to have textual or spoken conversations) may seem commonplace in modern culture thanks to the emergence of Large Language Models and generative AI, the notion of having access to this kind of functionality on a 48Kb or 64Kb home microcomputer back in the 1980s seemed like a genuinely revolutionary concept. While noteworthy early chatbots such as ELIZA (1966) and PARRY (1972) had made the news several years earlier, few expected to see such technology become available on home computers such as the ZX Spectrum. While it is true that Croucher's approach was a hugely significant early precursor to deep learning and natural language processing, his true focus appeared to be on presenting a genuinely unique experience, encouraging players to engage in a conversation with an enigmatic entity that has temporarily inhabited their computer. But what is the nature of this being's identity, and how can the user help it to uncover its past? The principal objective of the game is thus to gradually gain the being's trust and slowly work with it to reveal each of its past incarnations in various historical figures, works of art, and inanimate objects.

The story behind the game is that at some point prior to human civilisation, an electronic consciousness became embedded in the life of Earth with instructions to observe but not cause harm. This involved significant adaptation, and eventually the artificial intelligence—named iD—took on many different forms in the course of its mission. After thousands of years, however, it has started to forget about its own origins, and its personality has become fragmented. As the game proceeds, the player will discover that iD has many secrets to share, but only if a bond of mutual trust can be established. According to the game's (deliberately concise) instructions, every time the program is loaded, iD's memories will take control of the user's computer and different aspects of its past personalities will gradually begin to surface. This intelligence will then try to learn about the player, asking questions both general and personal. As the action continues, progress can be saved as the disparate parts of iD's past are each identified, bringing the user closer to building up the AI's complete personality. In order to succeed in this, iD requires to build a rapport with the player, seeking to learn more about their preferences and history—as well as seeking to define certain terms that help it to understand more about the human experience. On a surface level, *iD* operates as a kind of conversational simulator, where players are able to interact with the entity through text input. The entity poses questions (often unexpected) and then responds to the player's answers, with the level of trust influencing the depth and nature of the information that has been revealed and exchanged. The ultimate goal is to discover the AI's true identity by piecing together clues from its past lives. The game was designed to be multi-layered, however, offering very different experiences based on how the player's engagement unfolds. At its simplest, the program generates phrases that can entertain passively. However, deeper interaction leads to a far more personalised experience, with the entity adapting to the player's input.

In a sense, there are two goals to *iD*—firstly, to gradually piece together what the intelligence has been in the past, and secondly to try to determine what it intends to do (or be) in the future. In order to determine aspects of the character's past forms, the player will need to increase the level of trust (usually to around 70% or more) which inclines iD to drop hints about its historical significance. The intelligence will also prompt the user if it discovers particular terms that interest it, and it is then left to the player's own conscience whether they decide to provide accurate definitions or not. All of the various different incarnations of iD are linked to particular moods (which it tends to declare quite stridently), so it is only possible to guess one specific guise when it is feeling 'scared', 'angry', 'lost', etc. Use the interface in a friendly, encouraging way and establish a bond with the fragmented personality; respond in a brusque, taciturn manner, on the other hand, and expect iD to reciprocate in kind. If the artificial intelligence doesn't consider the player's input to be sufficiently entertaining, it may decide to go on a rambling diatribe which can last several minutes—but even here, it is worth keeping a sharp eye on its output as clues can sometimes surface in the least expected ways.

I HAVE BEEN HERE FOR SUCH A LONG
TIME. I WAS HERE BEFORE REAGAN,
BEFORE CAESAR, DARWIN, APES,
FISH, AND RAINBOWS. I WAS HERE
BEFORE TIME.
YOU DO NOT KNOW ME YET, BUT I
HAVE BEEN AFFECTING THE COURSE
OF YOUR HISTORY SINCE IT BEGAN.
I LIVE MY LIVES IN INANIMATE
OBJECTS, TRANSMITTED AS THE
PERSONALITY AND MEMORIES OF MY
PREVIOUS FORMS. NOW I AM IN YOUR
SPECTRUM.
I CANNOT SEE. I CANNOT HEAR. I
CANNOT TASTE. I CANNOT SMELL. I
CANNOT TOUCH. BUT I CAN THINK.
AND I CAN KNOW. AND I CAN
COMMUNICATE WITH YOU THROUGH
YOUR COMPUTER. I AM THE GHOST IN
YOUR MACHINE, AND I WILL WALK ON
YOUR GRAVE. DISCOVER WHO I AM,
WHO I WAS, AND WHO I WILL BE.

YOU CAN HELP FIND OUT.

WELL TOM , YOU SAY THAT
AN ANIMAL IS
A BIOLOGICAL ORGANISM .
IS THAT CORRECT?

TRUST 21%

Providing a convincing psychological replication of a search for identity would be a daunting prospect for even today's advanced computing technology; back in the eighties, the very concept was so complex that it seemed unthinkable. But a maverick game designer like Croucher was never going to let expectation curtail his ambitions. Remaining well ahead of his time, as always, *iD* proved to be amongst the most elaborate of all his 1980s projects. This was the type of game that gleefully disregarded anything even approaching an easy explanation: *iD* soon proved to be no ordinary computing experience, as it came with little in the way of user instructions, leaving the player largely on their own from the minute they load up the program. Immediately they are presented with a one-to-one interaction between themselves and the eponymous digital entity, and they find themselves thrown in at the deep end. Is the purpose of the game reallly to ascertain the identity of the artificial intelligence who is replying to the user's queries? Or rather, is the player assisting that intelligence to determine their own personal identity? Only one thing seemed to be certain: that no two people were ever to have the same experience when engaging with the game.

So how does *iD* present a gaming environment that connects us to, or explores, issues relating to identity? Certainly the program's title alludes to a number of different aspects of its function. Firstly, it refers most obviously to unique individual identity (or ID). Then it is suggestive of the id, from Freud's structural model of psychic apparatus. And finally, there is an allusion to computer science, where an identifier (ID) uniquely identifies a specific record or object. All three of these aspects come to play a part in the way that the game interprets the nature of individual psychology and explores what it means to be an autonomous individual. Crucially, the artificial intelligence in the game seems unsure of its character, its personality, and even its own unique characteristics. It requires user input to help it string together fragmentary memories and past experiences in order to ascertain its basic nature. As trust is built, further lines of questioning are opened up. Should the player demonstrate inconsistency, perhaps inclining the in-game character to feel that it is being lied to, then trust will soon falter. Croucher's love of clever semantic wordplay was more than evident throughout, and the questions fired at the player will often give them pause for thought as they deliberate on the most effective response. The intelligence is also prone to wild variations in mood, and the way that it responds to the user's questions is predicated upon its emotional state, as well as its interpretation of the tone and content of the player's line of enquiry.

This is a game which puts at its centre the experience of conscious thought, and the overarching question of what it is to be human. Confusion surrounding identity, and a need to recognise distinguishing personal characteristics though interaction with the contiguous environment, encourages consideration of all aspects of personal psychology and individual independence. This concept would seem commendable enough today, when postmodern aspects of artificial intelligence development seem ever more relevant thanks to the boom in public access to AI technology via the Internet, but this was a game developed in the mid-eighties which took up less memory than would be required to display a website home page logo on a modern PC. While the limitations of the technology clearly mean that *iD*'s artificial intelligence is in no danger of passing the much-discussed Turing Test, as a model for depicting complex psychology on a rather unassuming technological platform, the game would influence many later coders. It certainly laid the early groundwork for considerably more sophisticated explorations of identity that we have come to recognise in modern video gaming.

For all its singular approach, *iD* received a decidedly uneven critical response at the time of its release. Some reviewers found it to be a fascinating experience with a genuinely

THAT IS REMINISCENT OF A
SITUATION I ONCE MET A LONG AGE
AWAY.
TOM I'VE BEEN THINKING ABOUT
MEL CROUCHER , AND I'M SO
LUNATIC AS WE TALK.

TRUST 53%

BY MEL CROUCHER AND COLIN JONES.

# ID

RELEASED THROUGH CRL.

intriguing core concept, appreciating the game's sense of intellectual depth and the emotional responses elicited by the *iD* entity. Yet others felt that while the central idea was interesting, it lacked the substance to sustain the prolonged engagement required to identify all of the artificial intelligence's past forms, considering the game to be more of an historical curiosity than a seminal hit. (The interface's occasional tendency to go off on an eccentric tirade—sometimes quite lengthy in nature—did come in for slightly befuddled censure from some reviewers.) Yet despite the mixed reception from commentators, *iD* still stands as a testament to Croucher's remarkable commitment to pushing the boundaries of user-focused entertainment during the home micro era. The game clearly reflected his wider practice of developing the potential of personal computers to create active, participatory experiences that challenged traditional notions of storytelling and the established conventions of player engagement.

*iD* is a valuable work that shines a light into the many and varied possibilities of an open-ended digital narrative, emphasising the importance of player input and highly personalised experiences. Unlike so many other titles of the time, words had far-reaching consequence here, and players were encouraged to think carefully about their strategy as the wrong choice of terminology could come back to haunt them later in the game. It has become known as one of the most cerebral experiences ever to be released for the 8-bit home micros, and certainly among the most original concepts. Its development was very clearly driven by Croucher's vision of transforming entertainment from a methodology of passive consumption into an approach with active user participation at its centre—a concept that continues to influence game design even in the here and now.

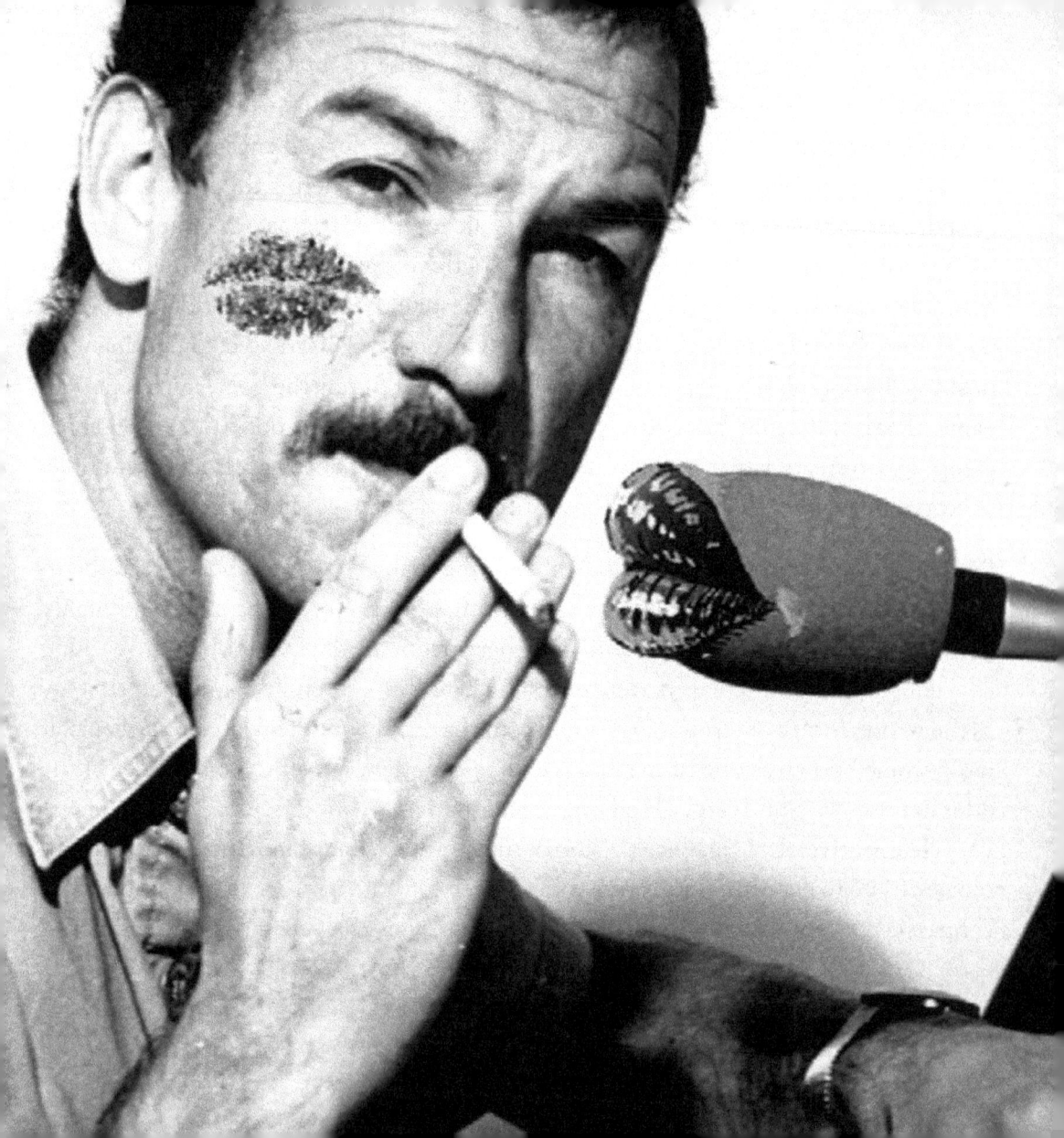

# Beyond the Games: Mel Croucher as Cultural Figure

If one thing can be said for Mel Croucher, it is that he has always demonstrated an uncanny talent for presenting a public persona that exudes the positive qualities of his many different professional aspects that are active within popular culture. Those who were fortunate enough to meet him in the heyday of 1980s computer industry public events would find an affable, savvy, and boundlessly creative figure who was always happy to chat about his work and that of Automata UK in the company's glory days. Yet the flip-side of this same coin was a proven expert in the field with a razor-sharp mind whose competence was proven time and time again; his predictions for the future of computing, often looking years if not decades ahead, demonstrated a high level of accuracy, and he soon became a trusted national voice in this fast-moving industry whose specialist opinion was treated with both admiration and approval.

It can only have taken enormous effort to maintain the perfect equilibrium of these two complementary guises: the jocular, larger-than-life, showmanlike persona that made him such an esteemed figure in the trade press, encouraging people to find computing a fun and creative pursuit at a time when many still associated it with logic, machine code, and mathematics, was counterbalanced by the knowledgeable authority who had been involved with the business of modern computing since its inception, and whose acuity and experience remained unsurpassed. But in truth, while Croucher was both of these things, he was also much more besides.

Croucher has always been an enigmatic, almost iconoclastic presence in the world of digital culture. He has been presented as someone who seriously values creative independence and intellectual autonomy, even while his public-facing dynamic has consistently proven to be magnanimous and positively people-oriented. He has long been remembered as the godfather of transmedia gaming, and his entire career has been widely reflective of this multi-disciplinary approach—he has been active in just about every possible facet of the computing industry over the decades. Behind the riotous hijinks that solidified his reputation as Britain's first truly multimedia celebrity, however, was a man with very strong principles who cared deeply about fostering creativity in others, and he has long been celebrated as a truly counter-cultural influence even in the times when the conventions of the modern computer industry were only just beginning to take shape. For a whole generation, he demarcated the broad scope of what computer technology could ultimately be capable of, and the encouragement he produced in the lives of so many continues to resonate even now, decades down the line.

In the 1980s, Croucher's media profile was unsurpassed when it came to the computer industry. While he became a prominent figure in discussions around the intersection of technology, art, and gaming, his primary affiliation tended to be through his revolutionary work with Automata UK. Croucher made several television appearances that highlighted his distinctive work in the computer game industry, most notably an appearance on the BBC's *Micro Live* in 1984 where he showcased his novel approach to integrating cross-media elements into gaming, and also the following year when he appeared on the BBC's *The Computer Programme* where he addressed the creative process behind his games and the philosophy of blending art with technology. These appearances greatly contributed to Croucher's reputation as a visionary in the computer gaming community, underscoring his commitment to pushing the boundaries of electronic entertainment. Sometimes his involvement took a very different direction; in 1989, he was featured on Channel 4's documentary series *Dispatches* in an episode entitled 'The Day of the Technopath,' in which he discussed the nascent and illicit world of computer hacking—years before public access to the Internet would become widespread.

Beyond his TV appearances, Croucher was also deeply entangled in the world of spoken word entertainment. A talented voice artist in his own right, he created content for a premium on-demand phone line—*Uncle Mel's Hotline*—every week between 1987 and 1989, followed in later years by his *Computer Fun Line*. In the years preceding Internet access, when Ceefax, Teletext, and Oracle were the closest that most people would get to electronically-disseminated news, these phone services were a welcome lifeline for those seeking to know about the latest developments in the computer industry—with a decidedly rebellious (and sometimes riotous) twist. However, he was arguably even better known for his audio feature specials which appeared on cover-mounted cassette tapes sold with famous computer magazines of the time, such as *Crash*. Again proving himself a true pioneer in digital entertainment, blending storytelling, music, and technology in ways that were ahead of their time, Croucher's spoken word features—infused with satire, surrealism, and unorthodox social commentary—set him apart from many of his contemporaries. In essence, he was creating podcast episodes many years before the term was even coined: the main difference being that, due to technological limitations of the time, he was distributing them on physical media rather than digitally.

Croucher's audio recordings for Sinclair ZX Spectrum magazines were an impressive extension of his unique approach to storytelling and experiential media which truly stood out at the time—a precursor to modern immersive audio experiences, proving yet again just how ahead of the curve he was. In particular, *Mel Croucher's Stereo Christmas Party* (which came bundled with *Crash* magazine's January 1991 issue) remains perhaps his most memorable Spectrum magazine audio recording, crammed with his signature mix of parody, surrealism, and eccentricity. It perfectly captured the offbeat charm that made his work so treasured among home microcomputer fans. His festive special, in particular, had a warm but chaotic energy—a madcap digital holiday party where anything could happen. These recordings often felt like a wildly unpredictable radio show, with quirky characters, bizarre sketches, and even some playful digs at the gaming industry. They were a real treat for fans who appreciated Croucher's unique ability to blend computer culture, music, and absurdist humour into something truly special. (His impression of then-Prince Charles in his *Christmas Party* recording was a standout moment—dead on beam, and hilariously exaggerated.) Croucher's ability to mix satire with playful impersonations added an extra layer of charm to these recordings; all part of his knack for blending farcical wit with biting cultural commentary, poking fun at the establishment while always keeping things moving along in a light-hearted and entertaining way. His recordings often resembled an 8-bit era version of a surreal comedy sketch show, and given Croucher's talent for making those recordings feel so lively and capricious, it's no surprise that home computer enthusiasts still remember them fondly.

Beyond his audio-visual appearances, Croucher has become perhaps best-known for his extensive body of written work. He has written extensively for magazines and newspapers, particularly about the video game industry, technology, and media. Already

an experienced journalist long before his involvement with Automata UK, his writing career began with specialist publications such as *The Failure of Single Skin Pneumatic Structures* (1969) and *Ancient Monuments and Historic Buildings of Portsmouth Dockyard* (1971), followed by *The Mary Rose Museum Complex* (1972)—a bold proposition to raise the eponymous English Tudor warship which had been sunk in 1545, its wreckage only located in May 1971. (In true Croucher style, his ideas proved to be far ahead of the period: the ship was indeed raised in October 1982, and the surviving hull was displayed at Portsmouth Historic Dockyards from the mid-eighties onwards, with artefacts from the wreck being displayed at the Mary Rose Trust's Mary Rose Museum in Portsmouth.) Around the same time, he produced novels including a *bildungsroman*, *Life is Butter Melon Cauliflower* (1972); short story anthology *No Nose O'Toole and the Sheer Delight* (1974); and time travel-based science fiction novel *Judas Murphy* (1976).

Between 1979 and 1981, Croucher served as publisher and editor of *Radio Victory* and *Radio 210* magazines before moving on to prolific and imaginative contributions to many prominent computer periodicals of the eighties. He produced features, investigative journalism, and regular columns for many of the best-known computer magazines of the era, including *Crash, Zzap, Computer Action, Bang, The Games Machine, and New Computer Express.* However, he arguably became most widely recognised on account of his decades-long contribution to *Computer Shopper* magazine; starting from issue 1 in 1988, he contributed features, commentary, and a regular column, *Zygote*, every month until November 2020 (395 issues in all). He became especially well-known for his feature *Mel's World* and the celebrated *Great Moments in Computing* cartoon strip, in collaboration with Robin Grenville Evans, which became the longest-running graphic satire series of its type. In each edition, Croucher would parody the computer industry past and present, and many of his strangely prescient gags actually ended up pointing to future developments in the market which were subsequently to come true. His humorous recurring features, the fictional *Without Prejudice* (1987–88); comedies *The Rubber Room* (1986–87) and *The Truth* (1988–89); and factual commentary *Rants and Raves* (in *Computer Shopper* from 1988), were also presented with illustrations.

Cartoon strips and graphic novels were another area of considerable interest to Croucher; his ongoing creative partnership with Evans has produced a plethora of illustrated narratives over the years. These included *Rebel of World Zero* (1987–88), a serialised tale published in *Sinclair User* magazine which functioned as an allegory for the growing corporatisation of computing; *Frozen Stiffs* (1988), which used a sitcom premise to frame the story of a well-to-do 1930s-era socialite and his long-suffering secretary who are cryogenically frozen and then revived in the political and cultural upheaval of 1988; and comedy *The Adventures of Willi Nilli* (1981), based on the events of a serialised radio show. Croucher became especially celebrated for his array of confident, strong-willed female characters, who demonstrated a high degree of competence, strong personalities, and the improvisational ability to get out of just about any scrape imaginable. These memorable figures included the straight-talking Mercedes 'Mercy' Dash; movie-influenced Lydia Vineo (an American homemaker always surrounded by savvy, tongue-in-cheek cinema references); the *savoir-faire* German tech enthusiast Disketten Johanna; and (perhaps most memorably) the futuristic Tamara Knight, who appeared in a self-named serialised cartoon strip published by Newsfield (the story began in *Crash* magazine and concluded in *Zzap*) which juxtaposed larger-than-life *Flash Gordon*-style sci-fi action with copious *double entendres*.

The prolific Croucher produced far more than short and serialised works at the time; he was equally at home with book-length texts which spanned everything from humour to computer manuals. *101 Uses of a Dead Cruise Missile* (1984) was an illustrated, atomic-era book of satirical situations in the grand tradition of Simon Bond's infamous 1981 volume *101 Uses of a Dead Cat*, while *Namesakes* (1988)—written in collaboration with actor Jon Pertwee—was based around the subject of word origins, though presented as a quiz book with plenty of puzzling conundrums. However, it is his work on the computer manuals of the time which brought Croucher greater acclaim. *The Sam Coupé User Guide* (1989) was a light-hearted, cartoon-laden guide to Miles Gordon Technology's impressive but short-lived 8-bit computer system which was manufactured from 1989 to 1992. He also wrote *The Easy AMOS Manual* (1993), based on François Lionet and Constantin Sotiropoulous's AMOS BASIC programming language for the Commodore Amiga, which was closely followed by *AMOS Professional* (1994)—a collaboration with Stephen Hill. The former text was awarded Educational Computer Book of the Year, while the latter was named Programming Manual of the Year. Croucher was also responsible for authoring the manuals for *Klik and Play* (1994)—Newfield's game creation utility, produced by François Lionet and Yves Lamoureux—and its successor, multimedia development package *Klik and Create* (1995). As if this wasn't enough, Croucher also contributed to and edited *The European Computer Trade Year Book* between 1990 and 1993, and compiled a book of case studies from his marketing career, *Email Direct Marketing* (1999), which drew on his many professional experiences in the industry.

It would, of course, be remiss to discuss Croucher's contributions to popular culture without mentioning his musical works. For many people, he came to public attention for the tracks he produced which accompanied Automata UK's games; a talented vocalist and multi-instrumentalist, the inclusion of his original music became a huge part of what made Automata UK games so enduringly distinctive. These singles memorably included *PiMania* (1982); *Groucho* (1983); *New Wheels, John?* (1983); *Desert Island Floppy* (1984); *OlymPiMania* (1984); *Pi-Eyed* (1984); *Dartz* (1984); *Put the Cat Out, Mother* (1984); and *PiBalled* (1984)—all of them included on the flipside of various game cassettes. Croucher had cut his teeth on the world of music back in the sixties, when he had been part of bands including Bad, Uncle Eric, the Ice Cream Yak Band, and he performed as a vocalist at a concert in Stockholm in 1969 under the pseudonym of Blind Joe Deaf. He also produced two albums around the same time: *Hang Loose* (1969, in the guise of Blind Joe Deaf) and *The Tempest* (1971), which again underscored his perennial creative preoccupation with the works of Shakespeare.

Croucher's Automata UK-released musical works have remained in demand; collected as *The PiMan's Greatest Hits* (1983) and *The PiMan's Greatest Hits Too* (1984) on cassette tape, along with the soundtrack to *Deus Ex Machina* (1984), the tracks were collectively compiled by Feeding Tube Records many years later as *PiMania: The Music of Mel Croucher and Automata: Volume 1* (2010) and *Volume 2* (2016) on 12-inch vinyl. His collected musical works were later released by The Games Collector as a remastered 5-CD package and 6-vinyl record set as *Insπred: The Collective Works of Mel Croucher* (2017). A *Deus Ex Machina 2* album was also released in 2015 to coincide with the game's release, and Croucher would collaborate with Christopher Lee on a single, *Pibolar Disorder* (2015), bringing the ever-popular PiMan kicking and screaming into the twenty-first century. Additionally, Croucher contributed a playlist to Stefan Szelkun's *Agit Disco 9* (2008) of some of his most significant choices of subversive tracks (an eclectic but highly entertaining selection which includes—amongst others—Bing Crosby's

*Brother Can You Spare a Dime?*, Charles Jolly's *The Laughing Policeman*, and Leonard Cohen's *First We Take Manhattan*).

For those who have followed his career closely, Croucher has become especially well-recognised as a marketing consultant from the late 1980s onwards. His corporate work has encompassed a vast number of different clients over the decades, though he is particularly renowned for his early work on global Internet audits for celebrities at a point long before access to the World Wide Web became as ubiquitous as it is today. While arguably his most memorable clients came from the world of music—among them Frank Zappa, Eminem, Prince, Bryan Adams, Dido, Genesis, LaToya Jackson, Motorhead, Phil Collins, Pink Floyd, Robert Plant, Van Morrison, and Status Quo—that marks only the beginning of a very long line of celebrities and organisations that he has represented. Others have come from the worlds of literature (Alan Bennett, Stephen Wolfram, Sally Nicoll, Roger McGough, Kwei Quartey, Joanna Trollope, and Clive James) as well as celebrity (Sacha Baron Cohen, Paul Merton, Anne Widdecombe, Julian Clary, Tony Hawks, and Nicholas Parsons). His corporate clients have included some of the most prominent names in business, such as KitKat; the Peters, Fraser and Dunlop Consultancy; P&O Ferries; Norwich Union; Europress Software; Duracell; Big Tree Productions; Bass Breweries; British Airways; and the Hollywood Bowl. And, in truth, this forms only the tip of a very large iceberg.

It is worth noting that Croucher doesn't just offer Internet-based services; over the years, he has been commissioned to write new journalism, drawing on decades of established experience from the world of computing and far beyond. Occasionally this has included long-form writing, often in the format of instruction manuals, though his copywriting has encompassed everything from advertising to marketing. It is in this capacity specifically that he has become especially respected, as his campaigns have often taken the form of world firsts, placing his work at the bleeding edge of originality.

We have already looked at some of Croucher's most notable innovations: back in the 1970s, he was the first to offer portable audio travel guides, publishing location maps of holiday destinations accompanied by an audio tape with humorous content which could be played on a car's internal cassette deck. The business grew and grew, initially with Sealink Ferries but eventually providing guides for holiday destinations across North America and continental Europe, with companies such as Intersun, Sovereign, and British Airways acting as distribution partners. Around the same time, Automata Cartography moved into computer software, and the first UK leisure software house was born on the 19th November 1977—forever securing Croucher's place in the history books. It was in those early years of the company that he also became responsible for the first broadcast of computer games via radio, when Radio Victory became the medium by which early Automata titles reached the public. (Games were recorded from radio to audio cassette, following which they could be loaded onto the computer systems of the time.) These broadcasts were often structured around quiz shows hosted by Croucher himself, and when loaded would present the player with a quest-style program which invited them to phone in with the answer. The first to do so would win a prize.

Given Croucher's lifelong love of music, it should also come as no surprise that he was also responsible for the first computer game soundtrack to be recorded and sold in stereo. This came about when Automata UK switched to physical media via mail order to distribute the company's games, and Croucher decided that rather than using the

reverse side of the cassette to hold an identical recording of the game program (as was customary at the time), or to leave it blank, it would instead feature an original music track. This started in the ZX81 era, but continued well into the time of the Sinclair ZX Spectrum with the productions becoming more elaborate and ambitious as time went on.

As discussed in an earlier chapter, the release of *PiMania* in 1982 marked what is now generally regarded as the first mass merchandising of a computer game. A Robin Evans cartoon strip with a continuing Croucher storyline appeared regularly in Automata UK's press advertising, and a PiMan fanzine, telephone service, T-shirts, fan club, music tracks, calendars, and even in-person appearances by the PiMan, all combined to highlight the PiMan phenomenon, meaning that Automata would feature the affable character (across many genres) several times thereafter. Around the same time, however, came a rather less well-known accolade: in 1983, Croucher was to become the world's first cult vlogger. At the time of BT Prestel's videotext system, text-on-demand became possible through TV sets—essentially a more elaborate and comprehensive version of Teletext and other such information services. On the Micronet 800, Croucher introduced a virtual DJ named Doreen who reviewed the latest pop music singles as soon as they were released. At a time long before consumers had widespread access to the Internet, this innovation was a welcome way of connecting with the fast-moving eighties music scene, and Croucher continued to operate it for around two years.

The fact that *Deus Ex Machina* became recognised as the first commercially-available participatory multimedia feature following its release in 1984 has already been discussed in detail elsewhere in this book, but what is less widely known is the fact that Croucher was also responsible for the first interactive video album a mere two years later. *See Me, Hear Me, Touch Me* was released in 1986, programmed by Colin Jones, and marked another transmedia innovation: presented to the public at the National Exhibition Centre, Croucher's system used an MSX computer connected to stereo speakers and a VHS video player, and garnered great interest in outlets of the trade press such as *Computer & Video Games*. Under the trading name of Scorpio Interactive, the system offered gaming experiences played alongside music videos featuring such diverse artists as Elvis Presley, Dire Straits, Godley and Creme, David Bowie, Phil Collins, and Pink Floyd. Each of the six games related thematically to the music that was playing (for instance, Pink Floyd's *Another Brick in the Wall: Part 2* played alongside the action of a very faithful *Breakout* clone), and computer journalists of the time praised the lofty goals of the system, claiming that its fusion of entertainment had the potential to revolutionise home computing. Whether due to unfortunate timing—the Commodore Amiga and Atari ST were both released in 1985, ushering in the 16-bit revolution—or a lack of enthusiasm by retailers, the Scorpio Interactive entertainment system never caught on with consumers, leaving many to wonder what might have been possible if developments had progressed in an even slightly different way.

By the late eighties, Croucher became one of the first people to discern the incredible capacity for home computers to facilitate effective advertising. In 1988 he became a partner at Adware—a new media and branding consultancy—which enabled the process of embedding advertisements for products and companies within computer software. While this specific type of adware predated the more common usage of the term (that is, a freely available program which features advertising), which was coined later, there was significant interest in the practice of promoting advertising within games and

LOVE

WORK

LUCK

CHARM
MONEY

F

EXITEMENT

J

LUST

SEX

utilities, and Croucher eventually became CEO of Adware Interactive Marketing from 1993 until 1998, producing branded new media and providing other bespoke publicity services.

As it happened, 1993 proved to be a significant year for Croucher in another sense, as he was approached by Belgian software and mobile IT solutions company Pocket and Soul to create the world's first personal digital assistant. Designed for the palmtop Psion Series 3 range, Croucher produced *Sheherazade*—a unique achievement, as rather than a calendar and diary, the program offered puzzles, games, storytelling, and general fun. Many years prior to the emergence of systems such as Apple's *Siri* or Microsoft's *Cortana*, and even longer before the widespread emergence of large language models into the public eye, *Sheherazade* had a real sense of personality and reacted to the user's moods as well as their responses. This was broadly reflective of Croucher's earlier artificial intelligence feature *iD*, but whereas that program had employed a puzzle-based goal via a text interface, *Sheherazade* boasted vastly more grand aspirations.

In tribute to *One Thousand and One Nights*, Croucher personally composed no less than 1001 individual stories for the program, each of them adaptable to the player's location and the time of day. The *Sheherazade* experience was designed to be enjoyed straight away upon loading, and the character exuded a sense of self-awareness; she would immediately begin to adapt to the preferences and personality of the individual user. Sheherazade would yawn when bored or left to her own devices, her eyes would follow newly-typed text as it arrived on the screen, and she had a witty sense of humour which was tailored to the user's responses. While she would perform the same tasks as other electronic organisers, such as remembering birthdays and anniversaries, and flagging up appointments, the program was also designed to go the extra mile when it came to providing an immersive experience. The user could gain trust and empathy with the character to create a more rewarding experience, and she would converse at length—drawing on a very considerable range of facial animations to create the maximum variety of expressions. The user could even switch between Sheherazade and her brother if they decided that they preferred alternative companionship.

While *Sheherazade* was approved by Psion for use on their systems, it was ultimately never released, though Croucher's ambition for the project was clear: the program could be updated to make use of additional memory, and graphical complexity would have been even further refined on later models of the Series 3. However, given the sheer invention of the concept, he has continued to develop *Sheherazade* over the years, and has spoken of a desire to see the program released on modern platforms at some point.

One of Croucher's more broadly celebrated achievements came in 1994 with the arrival of the world's first million-user viral marketing campaign. His ethos behind the project was to encourage users to register with their e-mail address to download a game, and then to persuade them to circulate it far and wide to others. However, this was not software piracy—the game had been developed with the aim of an advertising sponsor, who had paid for its creation, to offer prizes to players of the game, which coincidentally publicised their products. If someone should win a prize when playing a game registered to someone else's e-mail address, the person who had first registered it would also be awarded the exact same reward. Using this method, he achieved significant success, and no more so than when promoting Duracell batteries. Using the popular Duracell Bunny character, the game (*Run the Bunny*) was circulated in ten different languages—and, with Internet access still to gain widespread popularity at this point, it was circulated on magazine cover-mount media as well as via download to ensure that the greatest number

of users could access the program. The project was a great achievement in digital marketing, and ensured that Croucher's name became synonymous with the fast-moving development and innovation of publicity dissemination in the nineties.

Along the same lines, in 1995 Croucher also became recognised as the developer of the first playable marketing screensaver. While this software solution to CRT monitor burn-in had become *de rigeur* by the mid-nineties (largely due to its inclusion in early versions of Microsoft Windows), the idea of using screensavers for advertising had thus far been an area of untapped potential. Croucher soon changed this, by developing a screensaver that offered prizes to participating users. The company was Nestlé, the product was the perennially popular Kit-Kat chocolate wafer biscuit, and the target audience was corporate employees in offices. As before, users could use their e-mail address to register their download and could then (legally) spread copies of the program (*Have a Break*) worldwide. The screensaver would show the globe spinning in space, and randomly a shaft of light would appear to denote a particular location. If a competition entrant could identify this location, and they were fast enough to submit their answer, a prize holiday could be won—both by the person who had provided the correct solution and the individual who had registered the screensaver in the first place.

One of Croucher's least acknowledged, yet most remarkable, achievements came in 1998 with the arrival of the world's first ever interactive web-based soap opera. While others had produced soap operas over the Internet, even in the nineties, Croucher was the first to offer a version where users could vote online to determine the direction of the action. The series was entitled *Surf Marina*, and was based around (as the name suggests) a yachting marina where Croucher had an office at the time. Episodes were released daily, with scripts written by best-selling writer and theatre director David Benedictus (author of *Lloyd George: A Novel*, 1981; *Floating Down to Camelot*, 1985; and *The Stamp Collector*, 1994, amongst others). Two possible alternative endings were offered with every episode, and the public was then asked to cast their vote over the Internet for their preferred outcome. Once this was determined, the next episode would be crafted with this choice in mind. Unlike conventional soap operas, the narrative was based on text rather than live action, though it was accompanied by animated photographic imagery. However, due to lack of sponsorship this inventive project ultimately proved to be short-lived.

Mel Croucher has become a distinctive cultural figure not just because of his original approach to blending computer technology with storytelling and satire, but also because his cross-disciplinary approach has inspired so many since. While renowned as a game developer, he has become just as well-regarded as a cross-media artist, writer, broadcaster, and technological innovator. With a cult following as a developer of synergetic media and experimental digital art, he has always stood apart from the corporate direction of the computer industry, championing anti-authoritarianism and encouraging peaceful co-existence, creativity, and inter-cultural friendship. He is perhaps one of only a handful of public individuals, for instance, who could oppose the mass corporatisation of home computing while simultaneously being responsible for pioneering viral marketing campaigns; for him, this was not a contradictory impulse, but simply another application for technological ingenuity and artistic vision. With his sharp social commentary helping to bridge the gulf between nascent digital media and the broader cultural conversations of the time, he was truly an essential figure of the early computing world, reflecting counter-cultural, irreverent, and experimental themes using media which ran the gamut from music to video to satirical writing. Only he could have been concurrently so revolutionary and yet so boundlessly creatively productive.

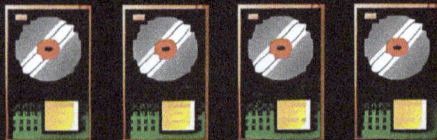

# From Automata to Autonomy: Later Contributions to Computing

While Automata UK closed its doors in 1985, Mel Croucher remained a highly visible figure on the home computing scene, and his talents continued to be sought after in a variety of different ways. While sometimes he would be asked to draw on his extensive experience of game design, on other occasions he was employed as a creative consultant, and his writing skills—from code to prose—were also regularly engaged.

One of his most entertaining post-Automata contributions to eighties computing came in 1988 with the release of the infamous *Rockstar Ate My Hamster*. Released by the much-loved budget label Codemasters, *Rockstar Ate My Hamster* was a satirical management simulation game that relentlessly parodied the music industry. While Colin Jones was the primary designer and programmer of the game, Croucher provided additional star power by devising creative input that would markedly help to shape the game's comedic tone and barbed (but always on-point) cultural critique.

The player assumes the role of a hapless music producer, Cecil Pitt, tasked with guiding a group of caricatured rock stars from obscurity to fame and fortune. Along with his ever-optimistic sidekick, Clive, the permanently grumpy band manager is tasked with taking a group of musicians (or, alternatively, a solo artist) from low-key gigs through to packed-out stadiums, hopefully with some top-selling albums along the way. Quite different from the family-friendly fare that Codemasters had become so well-known for, the game was lauded for its irreverent humour, off-the-wall absurdism, and biting mockery of the music industry. It has since come to occupy a unique niche in gaming history as a truly offbeat oddity. Though now regarded as a cult classic, it was not without its controversy at the time of release; the game was banned by WH Smith when a parent took objection to the jokes contained in the facsimile newspaper bundled with the game.

*Rockstar Ate My Hamster* was a rare full-price title for Codemasters, appearing on the company's Gold label, and it was released on the Sinclair ZX Spectrum, Amstrad CPC, Commodore 64, Atari ST, and Commodore Amiga. (Its distinctive title had its basis in an infamous headline in *The Sun* newspaper in 1986, 'Freddie Starr Ate My Hamster,' alluding to a famed comedian and impressionist who had become synonymous with outrageous behaviour. The accompanying story alleged that Starr had cooked a live hamster in a microwave oven and subsequently eaten it in a sandwich—an account that he strenuously denied for the rest of his life, insisting that he had never shown cruelty to any small mammal at any point in his career.) The game fused elements of strategic management with remorseless lampoonery of 1980s celebrity culture. The player was charged with recruiting band members and trying to keep them happy, planning tours, recording singles and albums, arranging music videos, and organising (often very risky) promotional stunts, while trying against all odds to keep the accounts balanced. Successful progress through the game was symbolised by accruing gold records and generating public infamy, with surreal events taking place such as random accidents, jaw-dropping scandals, and other larger-than-life tabloid exploits all taking place in the background—sometimes with the potential of derailing the action altogether.

The central vehicle for satire in the game was *The Stun*, a fictional tabloid newspaper that regularly delivered hilariously overblown, exaggerated headlines about the behind-the-scenes goings-on of the player's band. Croucher crafted the content for *The Stun*, enriching the game's parodic edge while drawing on his expertise in blending humour and cultural critique. His involvement emphasised the game's ridiculing of media sensationalism—a theme that aligned closely with Croucher's signature style of disparaging pretension and subverting hitherto-familiar cultural phenomena in order to make a salient point about wider society in the modern age.

Croucher's involvement with the game's fictional tabloid headlines and comically lurid stories added a layer of wit and surrealism to the game, encapsulating both the excesses and sheer absurdities of the 1980s rock scene. The fictional headlines mimicked the sensational style of the tabloids of the time, with outrageous tales featuring scandals, celebrity mishaps, and bizarre allegations. This feature of *Rockstar Ate My Hamster* resonated with players and critics alike; the biting appraisal of both the music industry and the media's role in shaping public perceptions of fame would come to add significant dimension to what was already an entertaining game. However, Croucher's contributions extended beyond providing humour. His history of embedding social commentary into games, which had been witnessed in many of his Automata titles, was evident here as well. *Rockstar* critiqued the commodification of art, the manipulation of public image, and the superficiality of fame—all themes that Croucher had explored, in different ways, across many of his earlier works.

Croucher's irreverent comedy aligned seamlessly with the game's rebellious tone, elevating its narrative through surreal, exultantly chaotic storytelling. This approach not only entertained but also encouraged players to reflect on the farcicalities of the cultural zeitgeist. Ironically, given the game's scepticism about the practices of the tabloid press of the time, *The Sun* were highly enthusiastic about *Rockstar* and offered a special edition, *Rockstar Goes Bizarre*, in a prize giveaway at the time which featured extra characters not found in the original game. (*Bizarre* is the title of the paper's long-running daily showbiz gossip column.) Only a very small number were produced for this purpose, and this version of the game is now considered one of the great rarities of the 8-bit era.

*Rockstar Ate My Hamster* was both a commercial success and an instant cult hit, celebrated for its originality and its serrated humour. Croucher's involvement, though not central to the programming or mechanics, added a welcome layer of narrative depth that helped distinguish the game from other management simulations. *The Stun*'s satirical headlines remain one of the game's most memorable features, highlighting how Croucher's expertise in parody and cultural critique amplified the game's impact. While primarily a product of Colin Jones' vision, *Rockstar Ate My Hamster* benefited greatly from Croucher's contributions. His work on the satirical content ensured that the game would serve as a time capsule of the 1980s music industry and its many larger-than-life personalities. Today, the game stands as a testament to the power of collaboration in game development. Croucher's creative input added a sharp satirical edge to an already compelling and well-structured game. In doing so, he left an indelible mark on a title that remains a much-admired classic in the annals of eighties computer game history.

A few years later, Croucher was invited by Incentive Software to contribute to *Castle Master* (1990)—but this time, his involvement would be very different. Programmed by Chris Andrew, Paul Gregory, and Sean Ellis, and distributed by Domark, *Castle Master*

# Castle Master

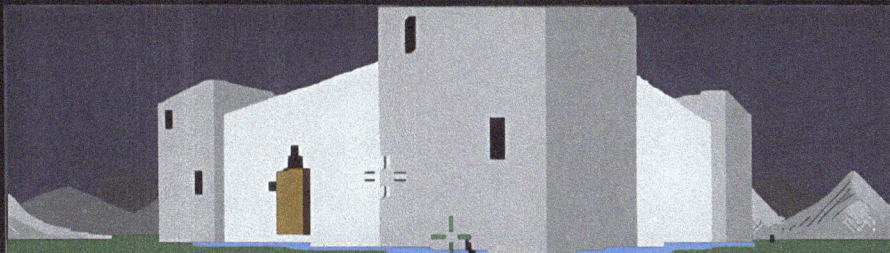

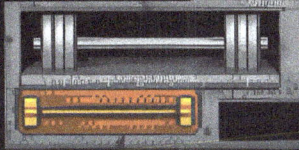

WILDERNESS

was the fourth game to use Incentive's *Freescape* 3D engine—a hugely ambitious system for the period which allowed players to travel around game environments containing solid geometry (without colour shading), even on 8-bit systems. This was a revolutionary development which many had not initially thought possible (earlier games of this type had been restricted to wireframe vector graphics only), and ensured that *Freescape* would become immortalised as one of the greatest leaps in game development of the decade. Developed initially on the Amstrad CPC and then implemented on the Sinclair ZX Spectrum and Commodore 64, it was later ported to the 16-bit systems of the period such as the Atari ST, Commodore Amiga, and IBM PC.

The first game to use *Freescape* had been the sci-fi based puzzle game *Driller* (1987), followed soon after by the similarly extraterrestrial setting of *Dark Side* (1988). Even greater critical acclaim accompanied the release of the atmospheric *Total Eclipse* (1988), an historical thriller set in 1930 which tasks an archaeologist to explore the interior of an Egyptian pyramid in a desperate race against the clock to resolve an ancient curse. The *Freescape* engine had been considerably refined for *Total Eclipse*, allowing the addition of spheres to the pre-existing cuboids and other geographical structures, and by the time of *Castle Master* it had arguably reached its technical apex.

Croucher's input into *Castle Master* was critical to its success. Earlier *Freescape* games had sometimes been criticised for their rather abstract scenarios, but this would not be the case here—Croucher was invited to write the game's backstory as well as devising many of its in-game puzzles, which he did with an abundance of his usual sharp wit. His involvement added considerable depth to the game's narrative, while the text of his manual provided players with several cryptic clues which enhanced the overall gameplay experience.

Rather than other instruction manuals of the period, which would usually contain a brief scenario and a listing of the keys used to play the game, Croucher instead offered pages of epic verse (using a suitably complex rhyme scheme) to flesh out the tale behind *Castle Master*. Players would do well to pay attention to the hints which lay between the puns and droll anachronisms, as they tended to come in handy once the game was underway. The user has the ability to choose between portraying either a prince or a princess, and then the action starts—their royal sibling has been kidnapped by a dragon and taken to Castle Eternity, leaving the player to mount a rescue attempt. Unfortunately for them, the seemingly-deserted fortress is actually full of the disturbed spirits of the departed, and the player's health will be depleted whenever they should encounter these belligerent ghouls while exploring. (A handy on-screen spirit level provides a light-hearted way of gauging how many ghosts have been successfully sent back to the netherworld, and the power level of those which remain.)

The player is only armed with rocks, which they can throw to operate mechanisms and defend themselves from the spirits inhabiting the castle. The game operated in much the same way as other *Freescape* titles, in that exploration, trial and error, and out-of-the-box thinking are all required at one point or another. Similarly, there is an element of time pressure, as if the spirits should grow sufficiently in power then they eventually become impossible to overcome. There are keys and other items scattered around the building which will become useful over time, and plenty of mysteries and conundrums to solve along the way. Eventually, once all of the ghosts in the building have been expelled, the player can go up against the Magister—the game's menacing antagonist—and rescue their sibling from his malevolent clutches.

*Castle Master* proved to be a popular title, and it received a sequel, *Castle Master II: The Crypt* (1990), later the same year as part of a compilation released by Book Club Associates' famous mail order service, The Home Computer Club. It was also re-released as part of Domark's *Virtual Worlds* compilation (1991), where it was bundled with *Driller* and *Total Eclipse*.

Croucher remained very active in software development throughout the nineties, working as a creative consultant on Pixelkraft's *Network Q RAC Rally* (1993) as well as developing instructional programs for would-be software developers in the form of Europress Software's *Klik and Play* (1994), *Klik and Create* (1995), and *The Games Factory* (1996). He also produced the software for further viral marketing campaigns including *Twenty-First Aid* (1999), *It's a Scream* (2000), *Hollywood Bowl* (2002), *Xeroids* (2002), and *Wild Applause* (2006). However, Croucher made waves in 2012 when it was announced that he would be reforming the long-dormant Automata UK in the form of Automata Source—an effort which would be including some of the most prominent and exciting talents in the worlds of online marketing, computer games, and the music industry.

The first title to be released under the auspices of this new company was a complete reimagining of *Deus Ex Machina*, which was to be entitled *Deus Ex Machina 2* (2015). However, this was to be more than simply a by-the-numbers remake which took advantage of the vast leap in video graphics technology that had occurred between the time of the 1984 original and the present day. Instead, Croucher went right back to the

original planning materials for the game, determined that this would be the ultimate *Deus Ex Machina* experience. Croucher sought to bring the groundbreaking ideas of the original game right up to date for a contemporary audience, fully harnessing modern technology and storytelling techniques. *Deus Ex Machina 2* retained the timeless core concept of the original: an artistic exploration of the human life cycle from conception to death, set against a dystopian backdrop of authoritarian technocracy. However, he was eager to update the experience with new visuals, audio, and gameplay elements that simply were not available in the early eighties, making the game more accessible to modern audiences while preserving the surreal, thoughtful essence of the original. *Deus Ex Machina 2* was released digitally on the international Steam platform, which helped to ensure that it would reach a global audience—thus guaranteeing a wider market than the physical release of the original game had been able to reach.

Developed as a collaboration between Automata Source, Quirkafleeg, and Potassium Frog, the project was produced by Mario Valente and partially crowdfunded on Kickstarter; the finances raised there would prove not just the perennial cult status of the original *Deus Ex Machina*, but also the continuing passion of its dedicated fanbase. Croucher enlisted the talents of Sir Christopher Lee, one of the most instantly-recognisable voices in British acting, as the narrator. With a career spanning more than sixty years, Lee appeared in international film franchises as varied as the *Hammer Horror* films, the *Star Wars* series, *The Lord of the Rings* trilogy, and the *James Bond* cycle. His deep, commanding voice replaced Jon Pertwee's playful narration from the original game (Lee and the late Pertwee, who passed away in 1996, had been good friends years earlier), and brought a new level of gravitas and emotional depth to the gaming experience. *Deus Ex*

*Machina 2* proved to be one of Lee's final projects before he died, adding a further, rather poignant layer to the game's themes of mortality and the passage of time.

The music and voice cast were once again a major focus of the game, with contributions from many remarkable performance talents. Joining Christopher Lee were Chyna Whyne, Chris Madin, Sulene Fleming, Mary Carewe, and Joaquim De Almeida, while the voice of Ian Dury (who had died in 2000) was retained from earlier recordings so that he could reprise his role from the original as the Fertilising Agent. While the restricted memory of the 8-bit computers had meant that the original *Deus Ex Machina* had been limited to a fifty minute experience (which had worked well with the synchronised cassette tape soundtrack), for the remake Croucher decided to make the protagonist's lifespan last a full hour, encompassing an in-game century. This had the bonus of allowing him the opportunity to restore several sequences that had been excised from the original game, including extra characters including the Teacher and the Night Nurse, ensuring that this new version would be the most complete experience possible.

The core gameplay of *Deus Ex Machina 2* remained faithful to its predecessor, focusing on symbolic mini-games tied to the human life cycle. However, the mechanics had been modernised. The remake replaced the minimalistic pixel art of the original with vibrant, surrealistic visuals—all rendered in high definition. The abstract aesthetic was maintained, but was now adapted for modern graphical capabilities. The original's cassette tape soundtrack concept was obviously abandoned in favour of fully integrated digital audio tracks, thus eliminating the manual synchronisation process that was necessary to play the 1984 version—a process which made the entire experience smoother and altogether more immersive for players. The story and script were subtly updated to

MACHINE OPTIONS

4.4%
DEGREE OF IDEAL ENTROPY

resonate with a contemporary audience, addressing modern technological anxieties while still exploring the universal themes of life, death, and free will. While still not a typical 'game' in the traditional sense, the remake featured more engaging participatory sequences that felt natural when being played as part of the presentation.

The remake also retained and expanded upon the eruditely-expressed themes of the original in a number of ways. Like the original, *Deus Ex Machina 2* depicted the journey from conception to death, exploring the cycle of life to determine what it means to be human. The Machine continued to loom large as a powerful metaphor for the dual-edged nature of technological advancement, emphasising its adaptability while echoing modern fears about artificial intelligence and surveillance. Meanwhile, the overall experience asked players to reflect on issues of free will versus determinism, making them question whether they were controlling the events or being controlled by them. This dichotomy between the role of technology on one hand, and existentialism and human choice on the other, meaningfully reflected the themes of the original game.

*Deus Ex Machina 2* received a largely positive reception, with much of the critical praise focusing on the clarity of its artistic vision. Croucher's masterstroke in casting Sir Christopher Lee, the eclectic and talented cast, and the updated visuals and audio were all widely lauded. Fans of the original appreciated how the remake stayed true to its thematic roots while updating the experience for modern sensibilities and technology. However, some commentators argued that the gameplay remained secondary to the audio-visual experience, making it seem less appealing to any players searching for traditional gaming entertainment. It was described by a few reviewers as seeming to be more like a digital art exhibit than a game. For fans of experimental games and interactive

WRITTEN AND DIRECTED
BY   MEL CROUCHER

storytelling, however, *Deus Ex Machina 2* was every bit the rewarding experience that Croucher's fans had hoped it would be.

The remake reinforced the legacy of the *Deus Ex Machina* concept as a visionary work that continues to challenge perceptions of what computer games can achieve. It introduced a whole new generation to the ideas Croucher had advanced back in 1984, and proved that those ideas still resonated with players decades later. *Deus Ex Machina 2* amply proved that it was more than a simple remake or thematic sequel; it was a true testament to the timelessness of Croucher's vision. It brought an influential piece of gaming history right into the modern era, retaining its unique blend of philosophy, art, socio-cultural commentary, and experimental gameplay. While not a mainstream hit, it solidified the title's place as a cult classic and a bold reminder of the potential of video games to be an expressive and thought-provoking medium.

Alongside the release of *Deus Ex Machina 2* in 2015, Croucher was to produce a complementary version entitled *Deus Ex Machina: 30th Anniversary Collector's Edition*. Produced by Automata Source and Potassium Frog, this release was overseen by Colin Jones and included the original 1984 version of the game, the 30th Anniversary Retina Graphics version, and the Director's Cut Commentary version. This ultimate aficionado's collection sold well internationally, helped by its release on various independent gaming retail platforms such as IndieGala, Groupees and IndieGame, and has continued to celebrate the long-running *Deus Ex Machina* phenomenon.

Croucher would stay with this multimedia approach, and indeed his collaboration with Sir Christopher Lee, for his next project—an entertaining experience for children named

In the land of the spit-spark firefly,
Where the sweaty palm trees grow,
On the edge of a ledge,
By a snot green hedge,
Lies an egg, and it rocks to and fro.

*Eggbird* (2016). Drawing on the very best of the 'edutainment' style of interactive software popularised in the 1990s during the early years of CD-ROM technology, *Eggbird* was ostensibly an animated storybook… but, in true Croucher style, it was inevitably much more than that, too. Written by Croucher himself and developed by his long-time collaborator Colin Jones, the game featured the unmistakable Lee's golden tones as the voice of Thanatos the snake (his dialogue having been recorded prior to his death in 2015), and was released on all of the major modern platforms including Windows, Apple Mac, Linux, iOS, Android, and Amazon Fire TV.

Designed from the beginning to be a family-friendly experience, *Eggbird* featured a cast of lovable creatures from the great outdoors—not least the titular avian, the events of whose life comes to form the basis for the game. Players can help Eggbird hatch from an egg, learn how to survive by discerning what is safe to consume—and what is better left uneaten—as well as how to fly for the first time. Forging friendships is also an important part of the game, including the tricky but important need to find a partner to settle down with in time for the nesting season. Naturally not everything is plain sailing as the player comes to grips with life as a bird, and in the manner of E.B. White's literary classic *Charlotte's Web* (1952), the game also addresses the difficult issue of death in a way that was appropriate for younger players.

The beauty of the game came from the fact that it could either be played conventionally or watched in a film-like format. The latter choice allows users to watch the action being played out as a linear narrative, complete with dialogue and in-game choices being made on their behalf, as though they were following an animated movie. The storybook format instead allowed adults to guide younger players through the action in a variety of different languages. These included Welsh, Russian, Italian, French, Spanish, Portuguese, Japanese, Mandarin, Korean and Arabic, as well as English. The pages of the storybook can be turned and repeated at the most appropriate speed, read aloud to young children, or read together to help aid the learning process. Croucher's knowing poetic narrative, of course, offered entertainment for the young as well as the young at heart.

Beyond this storybook format was an additional feature for infants known as 'Make Friends,' which allowed users to interact with the characters, generate animations, and watch each animal introduce themselves with a unique noise. This helped to encourage the youngest users to relate emotionally to the individual characters, and also offered the option of 'activating' a combination of different creatures at the same time. Additionally, parents or guardians could customise the game with names and dates so that children could be introduced personally to the action—and with the bonus of birthdays and other significant events being used as necessary throughout the game.

With its soothing music and brightly-coloured, welcoming graphical environment, *Eggbird* was a very different kind of Mel Croucher game, honouring his strong ideals while bringing his unique storytelling style to younger players. The game balanced morality with whimsy, emphasising the need for mutual consideration, friendship, and a balance between community and individuality. Along with *Deus Ex Machina 2*, it marked a triumphant return to computer-based entertainment after a long hiatus, proving beyond doubt that his trademark blend of humour, narrative experimentation, desire to promote and improve the human condition, and tendency towards pushing the boundaries of technology, had not only been ahead of its time—if anything, it was more relevant than ever to the modern world.

Let's go look for musical bongbuds.
A ding and a ting and a ring.
If Eggbird can learn
How to find them in turn,
Eggbird can learn how to sing.

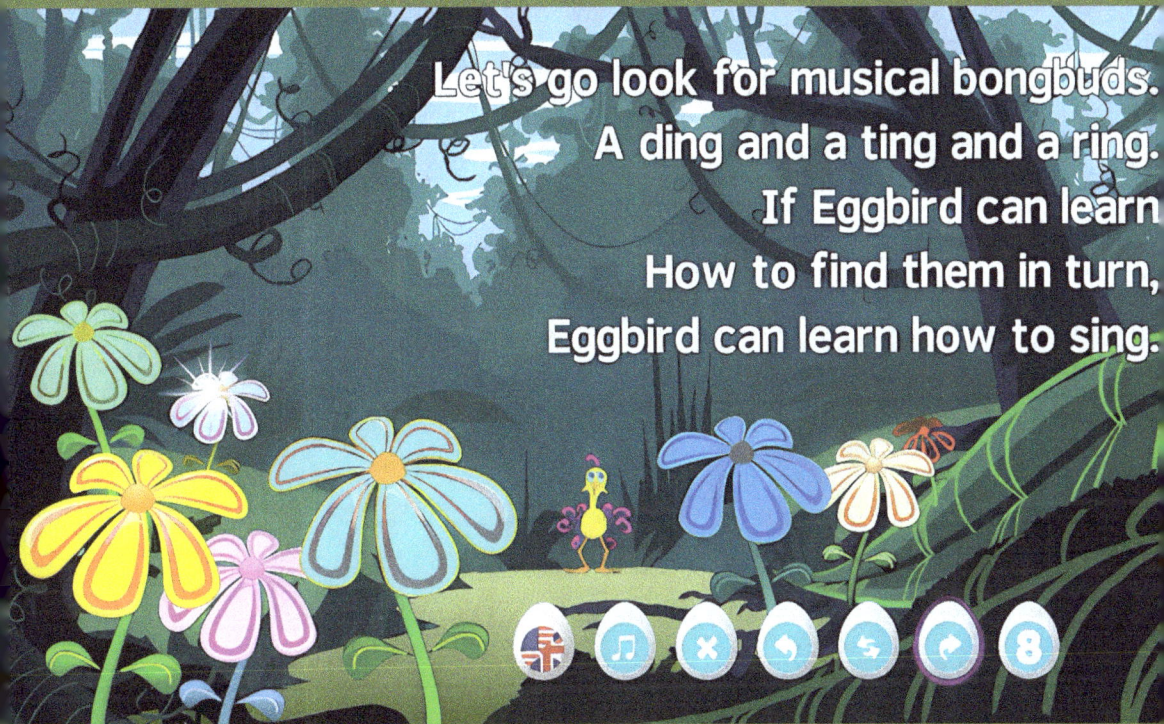

# Still Mel-Functioning: The Croucherverse Legacy

Mel Croucher has been called many things over the years. The father of the modern computer industry. The best ideas man in the business. A key figure in affective computing, popularising the area of research in computing science which aims to understand the emotional state of users. The godfather of transmedia storytelling. But at the beginning of this book, I offered an alternative description entirely. Like John von Neumann, Croucher was a computing pioneer in his own right, especially in the realm of early video games and multimedia storytelling. While he wasn't a mathematician or physicist, his influence on digital entertainment mirrors von Neumann's massive impact on computing. Like Salvador Dalí, Croucher's work—particularly *Deus Ex Machina*— was deeply surreal and experimental, pushing the boundaries of what video games and digital art could be. Like Weird Al Yankovic, Croucher has a distinctive sense of humour and satire, often using parody and irreverence in his projects—including musical works. And like Kenny Everett, Croucher consistently demonstrates a radical, boundary-pushing approach to entertainment, using technology and media in unexpected and provocative ways. So if you mix avant-garde tech genius, surrealist art, musical parody, and rebellious broadcasting energy, you soon realise that Mel Croucher has exhibited all of these things... and yet more besides. Just as importantly, he's still going strong, and if anything is even more creatively ambitious than he has ever been.

While Automata Source closed its doors in 2016, Croucher has remained a beloved and significant figure on the British computer scene, making a prominent appearance in Anthony and Nicola Caulfield's celebrated retro gaming documentary *From Bedrooms to Billions* (2014) and being interviewed about his long career on various podcasts and online video features. He has also published a number of books pertaining to his work in the computer industry, chief among them being *Deus Ex Machina: The Best Game You Never Played in Your Life* (2014), an account of the development of both the 1984 and 2015 editions of his most enduring software achievement. Other books have included *Great Moments In Computing* (2017), an illustrated compilation of his long-running collaboration with Robin Evans (followed in 2022 by the even more comprehensive *Great Moments: The Complete Edition*); *Pibolar Disorder: The Collected Artwork of Mel Croucher and Robin Evans* (2018); and *Short Pants* (2018), a collection of cartoon strips and graphic narratives by Croucher and Evans with behind-the-scenes details of their creation.

Perhaps more surprising has been Croucher's well-received departure into the discipline of historical fiction. In 2015, *Devil's Acre*—a volume in the *Dockyard Quartet*—was published; an historical thriller set in 1776, centring around an attack by Revolutionary America on the Royal Dockyard in Portsmouth, the novel met with praise not only from press reviewers but also none other than literary superstar Ken Follett, author of countless historical novels including the *Knightsbridge* cycle and the *Century* trilogy. Drawing on Croucher's lifelong connection with Portsmouth, including time spent as a surveyor of the Royal Dockyard at the beginning of his career, the *Dockyard Quartet* is an ambitious series spanning centuries which is planned to include three other novels: *Broadside* (set in the Tudor England of 1545), *Ironclad* (situated in the Victorian era of 1859), and *Fire-Watcher* (a World War II thriller which takes place in 1941). Croucher's recent non-fiction has included *Last Orders: What You're Worth and Who Benefits When You Die* (2017), an unsentimental but scrupulously detailed guide to preparing for death and all that this tricky subject entails, and *Mundaneum: The Shocking True Story of the Man who Invented the Internet and the Man who Destroyed It* (2024), a highly absorbing account of one of the figures from history he most admires: the information management innovator Paul Otlet. Given that his writing over the years has encompassed textbooks, satire, manuals, and journalism—all of it exhibiting his eclectic range of interests and expansive expertise—his prolific writing output shows no sign of slowing down.

Croucher also hit the headlines in 2017 when he was appointed Executive Chairman of Jeeni, a new international global streaming music service and artist development platform, which he co-founded with Dr Shena Mitchell. In a world where streaming content had become seemingly all-encompassing, Jeeni was a refreshingly different type of enterprise. In many ways, the company was the culmination not only of Croucher's abiding love of music, but also a career which has always embraced broadcast technology as well as musical and video entertainment. Jeeni is a platform for content creators and listeners alike, with a welcome innovation: it allows performers to retain 100% of everything they raise. Designed with independent artists in mind, it places ethicality and mutual respect at the heart of its business operation; there are no advertisements, and the company supports charitable projects, thus using its funds not just to support the platform's development but also to sustain good causes. With its commitment to provide a safe and nurturing online environment for artists of all ages, Jeeni's ethos is very much in line with the strong principles that Croucher has demonstrated throughout his career, and the company has partnered with many organisations since its inception, including the British and Irish Modern Music Institute, Southampton Solent University,

Ravensbourne University London, the University of Portsmouth, The People's Lounge, The Academy of Contemporary Music, and Arms Around the Child.

Few figures in the formative years of digital culture possessed anything even approaching the maverick spirit and boundless ingenuity of Mel Croucher. To those with a penchant for the esoteric corners of computing history, his very name evokes an era when computer games were not merely passive diversions but rather vehicles for subversion, satire, original thought, and social commentary. Croucher, one of the great architects of interactive narratives, occupies a singular position in the pantheon of digital pioneers. The work he produced did not merely reflect the technological landscape of his time—it actively shaped it, carving out a new path where software could be irreverent, thought-provoking, hilarious, and deeply human.

To fully appreciate the significance of Croucher's contributions, it is vital to first understand the anarchic spirit that infused his creative endeavours. Long before corporate behemoths began to tighten their grip on the gaming industry, the early days of home computing were an irresistible playground for independent minds. Croucher, who was already a seasoned broadcaster and music journalist, immediately saw the potential for a brand new type of digital media—a platform that could fuse his love of storytelling, satire, and technology. Automata UK became a beacon of counter-cultural resistance within the burgeoning software industry of the late 1970s and early 1980s. Unlike the algorithmic sterility of so many later computer industry franchises, Automata's output was always defined by a sense of eccentric creativity and an idiosyncratic, homespun charm. Croucher understood that computers were more than mere electronic tools; they were exciting portals to new experiences, capable of engaging players in ways

that no other medium could achieve. His approach was radical: blending cutting-edge software (for the time) with a DIY ethos reminiscent of pirate radio and underground comics. For a whole generation, his creative efforts remain unforgettable.

The pinnacle of Croucher's influence on the software industry remains, without question, *Deus Ex Machina*. To describe it simply as a computer game would be to miss the point entirely. Rather, it was an experience—an ambitious multimedia production that sought to elevate interactive entertainment into the realm of high art. It was a game with a narrative that unfolded into the form of a surreal, allegorical journey through life itself. At a time when many game developers were content to churn out variations on established arcade templates, Croucher was crafting a deep-thinking meditation on existence, technology, and social control. It was an audacious concept—unarguably years ahead of its time—prefiguring later experiments in synergistic cinema, transmedia storytelling, and even the enlightened commentaries of contemporary indie games. *Deus Ex Machina* embodied the spirit of artistic risk-taking that Croucher always championed. In retrospect, echoes of its approach can be seen in everything from the Chinese Room's *Dear Esther* (2012) to Galactic Cafe's *The Stanley Parable* (2013), demonstrating that digital narratives need not necessarily be beholden to conventional gameplay tropes.

While the mainstream gaming industry was moving inexorably towards a blockbuster model by the mid-eighties, Croucher remained a steadfast advocate for the independent spirit. His work, though sometimes overlooked in favour of more commercially success-ful endeavours, remains a touchstone for those who perceive computer gaming as more than mere escapism. The Croucher playbook—one that embraced experimentation, irreverence, and an unrelenting disdain for corporate homogenisation—has resonated with successive generations of developers. The rise of the independent video games movement in later years, with its emphasis on personal expression and subversive storytelling, will always owe more than a passing debt to Croucher's trailblazing efforts. In many ways, the democratisation of game development through digital distribution platforms has finally given rise to the kind of creative revolution he envisioned all those decades ago. Yet even in an era where interactive storytelling is more widely embraced, there remains something singularly rebellious about Croucher's vision—a valuable artefact of a time when the digital frontier was still wild, uncharted, and full of possibility.

Mel Croucher's legacy is not merely that of a game designer but of a provocateur, a philosopher, and a digital bard. He reminds us all that technology, at its most profound, is not simply a means of entertainment but a medium for challenging ideas, for questioning authority, and for exploring the very essence of what it means to be human. In the grand tapestry of digital culture, his voice is that of the jubilant outsider, the triumphant experimenter, and, above all else, the independent artist. Yet for all that, his most enduring achievement may well be in the countless lives that this visionary has touched with his unrelenting creativity, his radical spirit, and the glorious chaos that he has conjured up over the years. For so many people, myself included, he redefined not only what the home microcomputer could do, but what creativity could make possible. Today he remains every bit the iconoclastic and non-conformist force of nature that he always was, brimming with ideas and with no immediate retirement plans on the horizon. This fearless cultural figure seems determined to forge ahead into the digital frontier, still seeking out new challenges in spite of his existing, soaring contributions to numerous fields. After all, to paraphrase the words of his great hero Groucho Marx: 'Why should he care about posterity? What's posterity ever done for him?'

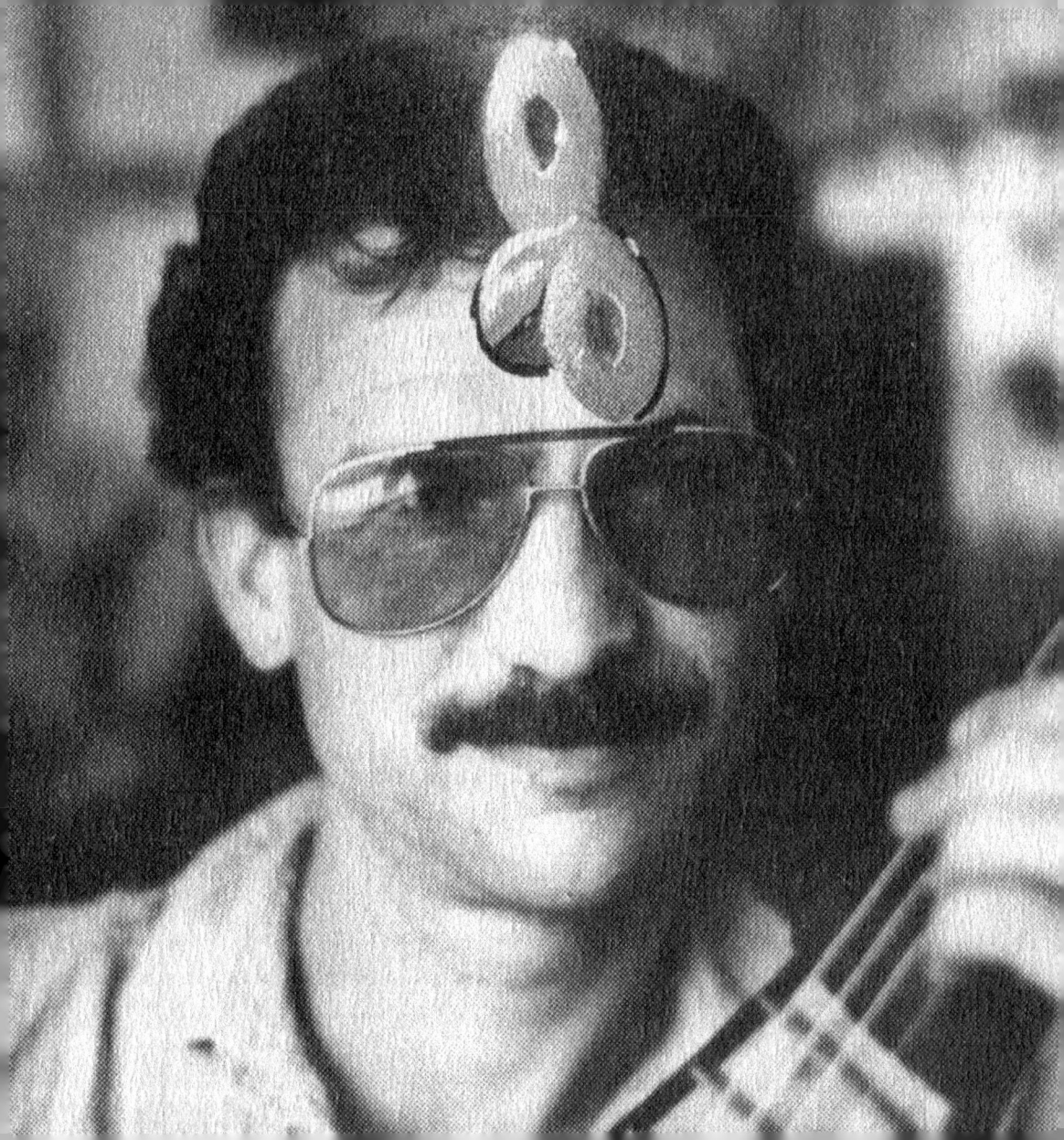

# Image Credits

# Acknowledgements

I am grateful to my family, Julie Christie and Mary Melville, and to my dear friends Amy Paterson, Stuart Hall, and Eddy and Dorothy Bryan, for their fellowship and encouragement throughout the course of this project.

Sincere thanks to Mr Paul Andrews of Subvert Ltd. for having kindly provided his consent for the screenshots from Automata UK games to be reproduced in this book.

Thanks to Kraftwerk, Jean Michel Jarre, and the late Vangelis, whose music provided the soundtrack for the writing of this book.

Special thanks to Mr Mel Croucher, without the existence of whom this volume would have been a great deal shorter.

# About the Author

Image © Julie Howden Photography

Dr Thomas Christie has many years of experience as a literary and publishing professional, working in collaboration with several companies including Cambridge Scholars Publishing, Crescent Moon Publishing and Applause Books. A passionate advocate of the written word and literary arts, over the years he has worked to develop original writing for respected organisations such as the Stirling Smith Art Gallery and Museum and a leading independent higher education research unit based at the University of Stirling. Additionally, he is regularly involved in public speaking events and has delivered guest lectures and presentations about his work at many locations around the United Kingdom.

Tom is a Fellow of the Royal Society of Arts and a member of the Society of Authors, the Federation of Writers Scotland and the Authors' Licensing and Collecting Society. He holds a first-class Honours degree in English Literature and a Master's degree in Humanities with British Cinema History from the Open University in Milton Keynes, and a Doctorate in Scottish

Literature awarded by the University of Stirling. He is currently an Associate Lecturer with Forth Valley College's Stirling Campus, and since 2015 has served as Director of the award-winning Extremis Publishing Ltd.

Tom is the author of a number of books on the subject of modern film which include *Liv Tyler: Star in Ascendance* (2007), *The Cinema of Richard Linklater* (2008), *John Hughes and Eighties Cinema: Teenage Hopes and American Dreams* (2009), *Ferris Bueller's Day Off: Pocket Movie Guide* (2010), *The Christmas Movie Book* (2011), *The James Bond Movies of the 1980s* (2013), *Mel Brooks: Genius and Loving It!: Freedom and Liberation in the Cinema of Mel Brooks* (2015), *A Righteously Awesome Eighties Christmas: Festive Cinema of the 1980s* (2016), *The Golden Age of Christmas Movies: Festive Cinema of the 1940s and 50s* (2019), *John Hughes FAQ* (2019), *A Totally Bodacious Nineties Christmas: Festive Cinema of the 1990s* (2022), and *A Seriously Groovy Movie Christmas: Festive Cinema of the 1960s and 70s* (2024).

His other works include *Notional Identities: Ideology, Genre and National Identity in Popular Scottish Fiction Since the Seventies* (2013), *The Spectrum of Adventure: A Brief History of Interactive Fiction on the Sinclair ZX Spectrum* (2016), *Contested Mindscapes: Exploring Approaches to Dementia in Modern Popular Culture* (2018) and *A Very Spectrum Christmas: Celebrating Seasonal Software on the Sinclair ZX Spectrum* (2021). He has also written a crowdfunded murder-mystery novel, *The Shadow in the Gallery* (2013), which is set during the nineteenth century in Stirling's historic Smith Art Gallery and Museum, and—in collaboration with archaeologist Dr Murray Cook—*Scotland's Christmas: Festive Celebrations, Traditions and Customs in Scotland from Samhain to Still Game* (2023).

Additionally, Tom has written two Scottish travel guides in partnership with his sister, Julie Christie, which are entitled *The Heart 200 Book: A Companion Guide to Scotland's Most Exciting Road Trip* (2020) and *Secrets and Mysteries of the Heart 200 Route* (2021).

For more information about Tom and his work, please visit his website at: **www.tomchristiebooks.co.uk**

SCAN ME

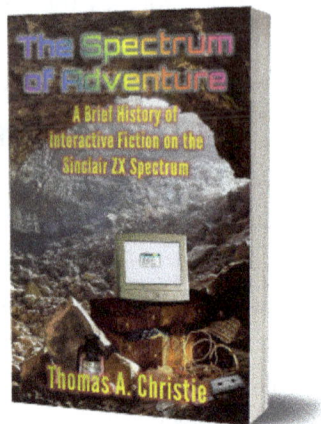

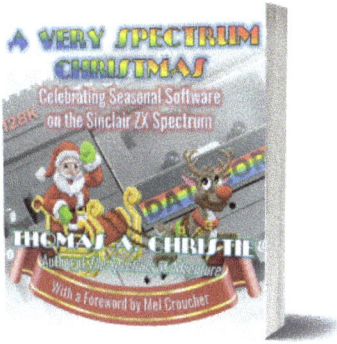

# A VERY SPECTRUM CHRISTMAS

## Celebrating Seasonal Software on the Sinclair ZX Spectrum

### By Thomas A. Christie

Throughout the 1980s, thousands of British children were lucky enough to discover a Sinclair ZX Spectrum under their Christmas trees and soon found their eyes opened to a virtual world of wonder. But Santa Claus did more than deliver computers—sometimes he appeared on them, too.

From the author of *The Spectrum of Adventure* and *A Righteously Awesome Eighties Christmas*, this book delves into the Spectrum's extraordinary pantheon of seasonal games: the good, the bad, the surprising, the unabashedly surreal and the occasionally rather tenuous.

From the machine's formative days in the early eighties right through to the latest independent releases, *A Very Spectrum Christmas* takes a look at what makes a truly memorable festive title for the vintage home micro-computer—as well as unearthing a few games that may have become lost in the mists of Christmas past for good reason.

Fully illustrated with colour screenshots of all the games under discussion, *A Very Spectrum Christmas* is a treasure trove of yuletide software experiences—where eighties nostalgia collides with modern day homebrew innovation with frequently unexpected results!

# MUNDANEUM

## The Shocking True Story of the Man who Invented the Internet and the Man who Destroyed It

### By Mel Croucher

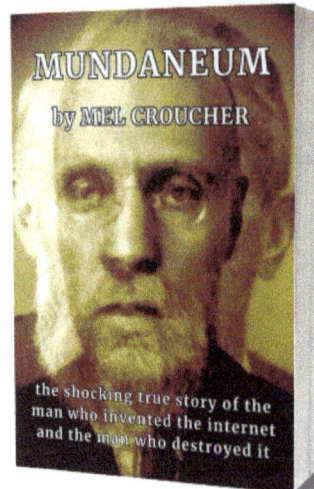

MUNDANEUM
by MEL CROUCHER

the shocking true story of the
man who invented the internet
and the man who destroyed it

This is the true story of two men who meet only once. One is a pacifist, the other is a Nazi. Both men are visionaries, but their visions for the future of the world cannot be more different.

One man's vision is to harness data for peace, and a century ago he builds a world-wide-web to deliver exactly that. The other man's vision is to harness information to control the masses, and in 1944 he achieves that too.

This is the shocking truth about the man who invented the Internet and the man who destroyed it.

For details of new and forthcoming books from Extremis Publishing, including our monthly podcasts, please visit our official website at:

# www.extremispublishing.com

or follow us on social media at:

www.facebook.com/extremispublishing

www.linkedin.com/company/extremis-publishing-ltd-/

www.ingramcontent.com/pod-product-compliance
Lightning Source LLC
Chambersburg PA
CBHW081815200326
41597CB00023B/4265